Failproof
Tactics
for Whitetail Bowhunting

BOWHUNTING PRESERVATION ALLIANCE

Failproof Tactics

for Whitetail Bowhunting

Tips and Techniques to Help You
Take a Trophy This Season

Bob McNally

Skyhorse Publishing

It has become popular—and rightly so—for many people to give something back. Often this is done by donating time or money to a university, or a foundation. It is fitting, therefore, that a percentage of the proceeds of this book go directly to the non-profit Bowhunting Preservation Alliance. This remarkable organization will use these funds to introduce the endless joy of bowhunting to new sportsmen, and expand and enhance bowhunting opportunities around the country. With the purchase of this book, every bowhunter has a chance to give something back to the great sport and tradition of bowhunting. For that I'm honored to be a part of this exciting and worthwhile venture that will help ensure that my children and yours always will be able to bend a bow for hunting.

Bob McNally

It's unusual that something you buy to support your passion will insure the source of your enjoyment will be preserved for your children and grandchildren. Save Our Heritage is simple: your purchase of this book will help us try to put archery into your community, will insure that bowhunting is offered to every beginning archer, and will insure that every bowhunter will have a chance to enjoy the great outdoors–with bow in hand–for as long as they have the passion burning in their soul. We appreciate your contribution.

Jay McAninch

CEO/President, Archery Trade Association

Skyhorse Publishing books may be purchased in bulk at special discounts for sales promotion, corporate gifts, fund-raising, or educational purposes. Special editions can also be created to specifications. For details, contact the Special Sales Department, Skyhorse Publishing, 307 West 36th Street, 11th Floor, New York, NY 10018 or info@skyhorsepublishing.com.

Skyhorse® and Skyhorse Publishing® are registered trademarks of Skyhorse Publishing, Inc.®, a Delaware corporation.

Visit our website at www.skyhorsepublishing.com.

10 9 8 7 6 5 4 3 2 1

Library of Congress Cataloging-in-Publication Data is available on file.

Cover design by Owen Corrigan
Cover photo credit Darrell Daigre

ISBN: 978-1-62873-683-0
Ebook ISBN: 978-1-62914-013-1
Printed in China

Dedication

For Chris . . .

The only date I ever had who gladly wore leaky, oversize boots helping to hang tree stands, while her lips turned blue from cold, and never once spoke about leaving for home, a warm fire, and supper. Our children are fortunate to call her "mom," for she understands the passions, joys, and intrinsic values found in a life outdoors.

Bob McNally

Table of Contents

Foreword

Whether you live in the Midwest or the South, bowhunt the conifer forests of the Northeast or the cottonwood bottoms of the West, you have the same questions about hunting for whitetails that just about everybody else has: What's the best way for me to hunt and what's the best equipment for me to use?

Through experience, some of us find our own answers, and that's another reason bowhunting is so enjoyable. But if you want to save a little time, begin here by reading *Failproof Tactics for Whitetail Bowhunting*. Author Bob McNally has assembled some of the best current information available on bowhunting for whitetail deer, as reflected in the conjured memories of experienced hunters—some of them famous, all of them expert.

Each chapter covers a critical topic of bowhunting. Former Olympic archer Jay Barrs, for example, examines the various disciplines a hunter must master to shoot accurately time and again. Joella Bates, a national 3-D target champion and veteran bowhunter, discusses accessories she considers essential to success; Ronnie "Cuz" Strickland, of Mossy Oak, provides his formula for quieting bowhunting equipment; Archer's Choice television show host Ralph Cianciarulo shares his secrets for hunting saddles in rolling terrain; and Michigan bowhunting legend Claude Pollington offers advice on ground-blind bowhunting. Most chapters involve a single hunter, but a few provide insights from a group, such as the chapter where seven bowhunters—among them, such famed archers as Pete Shepley, Bill Jordan, and Jim Crumley—expound on their "perfect" bow-and-arrow set-ups, and offer practical advice.

Among the contributors to *Failproof Tactics for Whitetail Bowhunting* are some hunters who are not well known outside their home range, but should be. For example, there's retired Jacksonville fireman Jim Jones, who has taken about 250 deer by bow on public land, including a number of record bucks in the 150-inch class. Collectively, the contributors have more than 1,000 years of bowhunting experience, and have taken approximately 8,000 whitetails with archery equipment. Famous or not, these guys definitely know their stuff.

Author Bob McNally knows his stuff, too, and is eminently qualified to produce such a book about bowhunting, as he is one of the most accomplished bowhunters and writers in America. Several Pope & Young-class bucks are among the more than 100 deer he has taken with a bow, and his numerous articles and books on a variety of outdoor sports mark him as a writer who knows whereof he writes.

As a writer cum expert, Bob is something of an anachronism—a hold-over from the days when the most successful outdoor writers were accom-

plished hunters themselves. We can thank Tom McNally, Bob's father, for that. I doubt that Bob ever thinks of hunting without also thinking of his father, who enjoyed everything the outdoors has to offer and made sure Bob had the opportunity to develop the same appreciation.

In the 1950s, Tom was outdoor editor of *The Sun* in Baltimore and later of the *Chicago Tribune*, as well as a major contributor to *Outdoor Life* and *Field & Stream* magazines. He had a lot of contacts and a lot of invitations to hunt good places, and made the most of them. From the time Bob started tagging along with his dad to hunting camps in Pennsylvania, to the moment when, as a teenager, he killed his first deer (a doe) in Wisconsin, Bob absorbed every crumb of information provided by Tom and his hunting buddies.

Among them was Fred Bear, whom the senior McNally had met at a Midwest sports show. When the two got together, Tom liked to talk about his bowhunting adventures with his longbow, and Bear like to talk about fishing for trout back home on Michigan's AuSable River.

"Dad helped Fred with his trout fly-rodding and Fred helped dad with his bowhunting," Bob recalls. "I was brought into the fold in the early 1960s. Fred Bear gave me my first bow about then, a recurve made for a youngster, and I started shooting it with Dad while he practiced for his Midwestern deer hunts and two African bowhunts he made in the mid-1960s."

Bob was a quick study. By 1964, he was strong enough to shoot a Bear Kodiak recurve, a 50-pounder, matched with cedar arrows and Bear Razorheads. It was on one of their bowhunting forays in central Wisconsin that Bob got that first deer, in 1965, when he was 15 years old, while hunting from the ground. He was on his way.

As soon as Bob was old enough to get a driver's license the following year, he began bowhunting throughout the Midwest. He shot his first buck, a six-pointer, when he was 16, also while hunting from the ground. Remember, this was in the days when tree stands were illegal in a lot of states, including Wisconsin, and there was no designer camouflage nor even cover scents (except for pine tar, of course).

By the time Bob enrolled in the University of Wisconsin, he was a veteran bowhunter. Even then, Wisconsin was an archer's heaven. Everyone hunted whitetails, and trophy-class bucks seemed to be everywhere. Bob got his share of trophies, but he also began to expand his hunting horizons to other states. During those early, pivotal days of bowhunting in the late 60s and early 70s, the McNallys made annual treks to Montana to hunt near the family vacation house in the bottomlands of the Madison River. Mule deer and whitetails were on the menu. Bob and friends traveled to Michigan and Illinois to bowhunt until, after graduation, he moved to Florida to become outdoors editor of the *Florida Times-Union* in Jacksonville. Living in the South, with its long archery seasons and extremely liberal deer limits, suited Bob to a T.

He hit the Sunshine State about the same time compound bows started registering with bowhunters nationwide. By 1978, Bob had abandoned recurves for compounds, shooting with sights rather than instinctively, and had switched from a shooting glove to a tab. Ten years and a few dozen deer later, Bob had changed to a release aid and was slinging carbon shafts as frequently as he was using aluminum arrows.

Bob has been a bowhunter for more than 40 years, and still maintains the same enthusiasm for the sport that he first felt back when his father let him tag along on hunts with his famous friends. Better yet, Bob, like his dad, is a great motivator himself, which explains why his sons Eric and Matt are dedicated bowhunters.

One thing that years of bowhunting experience have taught Bob is that most bowhunters are bedeviled by common problems: how to set up a bow for maximum efficiency; how to formulate various hunting strategies based on food sources, seasonal patterns, and weather factors; how to blend into a deer's environment unobtrusively; how to make the right choices. Answers to such questions are found in the following pages.

Bob selected the range of topics covered in *Failproof Tactics for Whitetail Bowhunting* well, and his choice of contributors is equally impressive. Sharing campfires and tales with such men and women through the years, Bob has absorbed much about the science of hunting and the character of great hunters, and knows how valuable their insights can be to others.

The advance in archery technology has leveled the playing field in terms of allowing even casual archers to be excellent shots, but there is more to being a consistently productive bowhunter than shooting skill. In some hunters, there is a spark that flames into a quest for excellence over time. These are the archers who begin their hunting careers on equal footing with the rest of us, but somewhere along the trail, they split off from the pack. They become better. They raise their own bars higher and settle for nothing less. They achieve.

You can read what they have to say in *Failproof Tactics for Whitetail Bowhunting* just because it is interesting, but you will also learn something of how to be like them. Many of the contributors are the bowhunting super-stars of today, and much of what they have to teach will mold the superstars of bowhunting's tomorrow. The tactics and techniques you'll read about in this book might help you become one of them.

Colin Moore

Introduction
The Whitetail Boom

Dozens of books have been written about bowhunting whitetail deer. And every year, hundreds of magazine articles are dedicated to the same subject.

So why another archery deer hunting book?

Because the sport continues to blossom, as whitetail deer have expanded throughout America. Today, there are whitetails in places where there were few only a decade ago . . . more and larger bucks than ever before. As deer populations expand, and herd conditions improve, more people are drawn to whitetail hunting and, in turn, bowhunting.

Whitetails are so numerous that a large percentage of deer hunters collect venison with little trouble each season. Thus the challenge to simply "take a deer" with a firearm is not what it once was, which has also given the close-quarters and difficult game of bowhunting a surge in popularity.

"I grew up when there were almost no deer," says Bill Jordan of Columbus, Georgia, developer of Realtree Camouflage, television host, and a bowhunter with dozens of great bucks to his credit. "But about 25 years ago, whitetail populations really came on strong, and in just a few years I'd taken plenty with my rifle. So I looked for a new challenge, and bowhunting filled the order."

Jordan says it's easy to put his rifle crosshairs on a buck at 100 yards and pull the trigger—at least compared to taking that deer with a bow and arrow. In bowhunting, everything is so close. The stand must be positioned very near a deer—preferably within 20 yards. The wind must be right. Camouflage perfect. A hunter can't move. There can be no mistakes. None.

"Even when an ambush for a deer turns out just right and a bowman gets his arrow drawn, there's still no sure thing," Jordan says with a knowing smile. "It's still very easy to miss a deer with a bow, much easier than with a rifle or shotgun. This difficulty, this challenge of taking a whitetail at close range, is why bowhunting is so exciting and fun for me.

"A bowhunter learns an incredible amount about deer in a very short time because the animals must be close for a shot. If I see a nice buck at 100 yards with a rifle, I'll take the shot at long range. With a bow, I've got to wait and watch that deer cover a lot of ground before he gets within arrow range. I know bowhunting has made me a better deer hunter. With a bow, I've been able to observe nearby animals make scrapes, fight, rub their antlers, feed, test the wind, and do a multitude of other things I never would have given them time to do if I'd been using a firearm."

In many areas with burgeoning deer herds, does must be cropped in large numbers to keep whitetail populations in check. For many hunters, downing a doe with a rifle is an anti-climatic event. But bowhunting offers such experienced sportsmen renewed reward.

"Our hunt club has too many does, so I thought bowhunting would be a good way to take them off the land, yet provide fun sport," says Mike Wroten of Switzerland, FL. "Bowhunting also lets me get into the woods earlier in the year, before the general gun seasons begin. I took three deer last year with my bow, and it was some of the most exciting hunting I've ever enjoyed."

Never before have so many hunters had the opportunity to harvest so many deer, during seasons so long, in so many different regions of America. In South Carolina today, whitetail deer hunting starts August 15, and in some areas sportsmen can harvest a buck a day (plus does, with

Many veteran deer hunters gain a whole new enthusiasm for the sport when they pick up a bow. Even harvesting does is a heart-pounding adventure.

proper tags) through a season that ends December 31. It's much the same in Alabama, where archers head afield in mid-October and can lawfully take one deer of each sex through January 31.

Georgia, Mississippi, Louisiana, and Florida have similar liberal hunting regulations, but don't think the deer boom is confined to the South. It's happening in the East, North, and out West, where whitetails are rapidly taking over traditional mule-deer ranges.

I grew up in Illinois, and that state's first modern-day deer hunting season in 1957 is still vivid in my mind, because my father downed an incredible 23-point non-typical southern Illinois buck, nearly making the Boone & Crockett record book. It was the first real deer I ever saw and touched, and I was completely awestruck.

I always remember a lot of deer in Illinois and in nearby Wisconsin, Indiana, Minnesota, and Michigan. But even in those states, the whitetail explosion has been nothing less than phenomenal over the past two decades. I visit the Midwest today, and can hardly believe there are even more deer there now than I recall from my beginning deer-hunting days.

In Illinois 35 years ago, for example, a very restrictive lottery system for resident deer tags was in effect. It was a lucky man who got a county-only hunting permit, and he was luckier still if he filled it with a deer, let alone a buck. While there were virtually no deer there at the turn of the century, the state now has an estimated population of 750,000 whitetails, with an annual hunter harvest of 150,000 animals.

Those are staggering numbers—a larger whitetail population and hunter harvest than I ever thought Illinois could produce.

Remarkably, Wisconsin and Michigan have gone way beyond the numbers of deer I remember from my earliest days as a Midwest hunter. In Michigan in 2002, an estimated 1.75 million deer walked the state, and that year hunters harvested 432,000 whitetails! The bulk of those deer were taken during a comparatively short 15-day rifle season.

In a typical Michigan archery season, more than 300,000 bowmen collect over 125,000 whitetails. Today in Michigan, deer hunters harvest more whitetails in a single season than the number of deer that resided in the entire state in 1960!

The story is similar in the Badger State, where only 30 years ago hunters were taking just over 100,000 deer per year. In 2002, Wisconsin sportsmen downed 372,000 whitetails from the state's estimated herd of 1.4 million!

Even in urbanized New Jersey, the whitetail boom is incredible by anyone's measure. There are so many deer in some areas that the state game department has made hunting fairly liberal. On paper, at least, a hunter could lawfully harvest 108 whitetails in a single year! A further telling statistic of how many deer the state must annually crop from its 150,000 herd: 42 percent of the gun hunters in New Jersey down a deer; 33 percent of the muzzleloaders are successful; and an impressive 21 percent of the bowhunters connect with whitetails.

Obviously, the good old days of deer hunting are happening today. But what has happened over the past 10 to 20 years to produce such incredible whitetail numbers? How could there be so many deer in so many places so quickly?

"It varies from state to state, but in Ohio, the reason deer populations have boomed recently is because of man," explains Mike Tonkovich, Ohio's deer project leader. "Deer habitat has improved tremendously over the last 30 years, and that has produced a lot of deer. In southeastern Ohio, there was a lot of farm abandonment in the 1960s, so there was limited food and cover. Today, farms are flourishing and there is a lot of successive growth of cover—perfect conditions for whitetails.

"Also, game managers in the state worked hard early on to increase the herd, with buck-only harvests. From 1966 through 1978, antlerless harvest of whitetails was very restricted. Antlerless deer permits were issued in large numbers only beginning in 1979, when managers believed herd control in some areas was necessary.

"Whitetails do best in 'fringe country'—mixed woods, brush, and agriculture—precisely what Ohio has right now. Ohio has reached the limit in deer population, with an estimated 550,000 animals, an all-time high, and an annual harvest approaching 160,000."

Kevin Wallenfang, assistant deer ecologist for Wisconsin, concurs with Tonkovich, but says there are some other considerations for the whitetail boom in the Badger State.

"Wisconsin has been setting deer population and deer harvest records pretty frequently, maybe too frequently," he laments. "In some regions in the southern part of the state, urban sprawl is taking over a lot of traditional wildlife habitat, and farms are turning into suburban developments, with forest preserves and parks. Wisconsin loses 50 acres of agriculture land every hour—that's less land available to hunting, but deer continue to thrive.

"Estate homes cover five-, 10-, 20- and 40-acre regions where, only a few years ago, hunters and farmers were taking their bucks every fall. On such land, a hunter or two may still take a buck or a doe, but that's considerably less harvest on the same land than a few years ago. There's also a trend with large landowners and some hunt clubs to control several hundred acres, and they shoot only a few 'trophy' bucks every year. This increases deer numbers as well."

Wallenfang says there's also a lot more Wisconsin property in CRP every year, which makes for superb whitetail habitat. And in much of the state, a decade of mild winters has limited winter die-offs.

Die-offs are the result of overpopulation, whether from disease or from severe winters. In a well-managed whitetail herd, with good weather conditions, they're rare. But sometimes Mother Nature deals a gruesome hand, particularly now that whitetail numbers are at modern record levels throughout most of America.

In the Upper Peninsula of Michigan, during the hard winter of 1995, an estimated 200,000 whitetails died from heavy snow, cold, and lack of food, according to state wildlife technician Joe Robison. The winter of '96 was bad, too, he says; "U.P. die-offs again were high. Yet deer are amazingly resilient, and the U.P. population rebounded quickly, since herds can increase 30 percent or more in a single year under the right habitat conditions."

In the South, winter die-offs don't occur, but disease takes its toll. The battle to eliminate the screwworm in the 1940s is believed by many state game managers to have been the primary reason for the surge in Dixie deer populations.

The screwworm weakened and killed cattle as well as deer, so the beef industry spent a lot of money on research and put the screws to the screwworm. Through an ingenious method of sterilizing male screwworms, the parasite was eliminated from the U.S. by the 1950s, according to Alabama assistant chief of game Keith Guyse. Screwworm infestation remains a cattle problem in Mexico and other Latin American countries.

"Timing of the screwworm elimination was perfect for Southern deer herds," Guyse explains. "At the same time, state game departments began intensive deer restocking, and land-use changes were under way, too. Today, in Alabama, Mississippi, Georgia, and some other Southern states, the ideal habitat mix exists for whitetails. There's pasture land and row crops, hardwoods, and tree farms with short rotations that regularly produce clear-cut browse. All these things combined, plus proper game management by using hunters as crop tools, make for a large and healthy Alabama deer herd—about 1.5 million animals today, numbers unprecedented in modern times."

One interesting theory about the abundance of whitetails initially seems contrary to logic. The concept is that maybe, just maybe, large and growing predator populations (primarily coyotes) over the last decade have removed many lame, sick, and inferior animals from the deer herd. This, in turn, has resulted in the strongest, healthiest, wiliest whitetails surviving and flourishing. The idea is that instead of predators reducing deer herds, as many hunters have worried for years, coyotes and other predators may actually have increased whitetail numbers.

The predator theory is not embraced by all state biologists. Yet Gerry Cooke, a Ph.D. and program director for the Texas Upland Wildlife

Ecology unit, says every South Texas deer hunter should "shake the predator paw of every coyote."

"In south Texas, coyotes have been a good and important hedge on overpopulation of whitetails, and that has resulted in a healthier overall deer herd, with better animals and more trophy bucks," states Cooke. "If big deer, and good bucks are your goal, overpopulation is deadly, and is contrary to sound management. So the coyote in Texas brush country has been very helpful."

The deer boom in Texas, like so many other states, however, has been primarily the result of land-use changes at the hands of man. Cooke says that in the 1920s and 1930s, the brush country that's now so famous for whitetails was rolling plains full of pronghorn antelope. But with the introduction of cattle and fences, and land management that benefited man and his beasts, the plains of South Texas became brush—superb whitetail country.

"Brush is marginal habitat for producing lots of whitetails," Cooke continues. "But the terrain is high in concentrated protein and deer survive well. This produces rangy, long-legged deer with large antlers compared to body mass—something south Texas landowners love, because the deer are an important cash crop for many people who lease property to hunters and clubs.

"Animals use habitat on a scale of resources, and it just so happens that whitetails use the same scale of resources as humans, so they thrive and prosper as we do. Humans impact habitat and natural systems, like bringing corn to Iowa, and deer thrive on that change. It's happened all over the country.

"This is why whitetails have pushed out mule deer in some Western habitats. As man has impacted the land, it has become more to the liking of whitetails than mule deer. Further, whitetails are much more adaptable and more aggressive in their adaptation to habitat change than mule deer."

This, then, is why whitetails have become far more numerous than mule deer in parts of Montana, Idaho, Wyoming, and Colorado. In one region of Montana where I've regularly hunted deer in river bottoms for over 30 years, whitetails now outnumber mule deer 50 to 1. Twenty-five years ago, the ratio was reversed.

Georgia senior wildlife biologist Scott McDonald agrees that the adaptable nature of whitetails has led to the species abundance we know today.

"Deer are not moving into suburbia, we are moving suburbia to where whitetails roam," McDonald explains. "There are plenty of good deer groceries in home gardens and flower beds. That, coupled with 'no hunting' signs that go up in such areas, can only increase deer numbers unless state game departments take active management in the system. In 1991, Georgia had an estimated deer population of 1.3 million. We realized more had to be cropped from the herd to keep it healthy, so we liberalized either-sex deer seasons, and have purposely brought the population down to about 900,000, which is just about right."

Many deer hunters know about the dangers of whitetail overpopulation, and the "carrying capacity" of the land: Any given deer range can only support or "carry" so many animals before Nature takes charge and animals become weak, sick, and die. But these days, game managers differentiate between "biological" and "cultural" carrying capacity.

"Deer 'overpopulation' is more a perception in New Jersey than a reality," says Dan Ferrigno, a biologist with that state's Department of Natural Resources. "Because of urbanization, and deer living in more backyards than ever before, many residents believe there are way too many deer. As a result, we have 'suburban deer management programs' designed to reduce whitetails in some areas, and also to help farmers with crop depredation. Five percent of New Jersey's farms have deer depredation problems.

"All this is what biologists call 'cultural' carrying capacity. In essence . . . the number of deer that people are willing to live with in a state or region." Which is not necessarily the same as an area's "biological" carrying capacity. "In New Jersey, we have 150,000 whitetails—about the state's 'cultural carrying capacity.' The true 'biological carrying capacity' is 400,000 deer—nearly three times the current state whitetail population."

It's the author's hope that readers share their archery knowledge with friends and family.

Paul Shelton, the DNR man in charge of the Illinois deer program, says the same thing is true in the Land of Lincoln.

"Years ago we thought we knew how many deer the land could support, and biologists offered numbers of whitetails per square mile as a maximum—carrying capacity, in other words," he explains. "But in many areas of the U.S., especially the Midwest corn and grain belt, and particularly in Illinois, we don't know what the true 'biological deer carrying capacity' of land actually is because whitetail numbers would never be allowed to reach those high figures. Public tolerance of deer is much lower in Illinois than what the land can actually support."

For many bowhunters like me, this is remarkable and exciting information. Thirty years ago, I thought places like Wisconsin and Michigan had all the deer the land could possibly hold. Today, those states have several times more whitetails than yesterday. And states like Illinois and Iowa, which just a generation ago had comparatively few deer, are now bursting with bucks. To think that they could "biologically" accommodate even more whitetails boggles the mind.

It's all great news to bowmen, who are allowed to hunt urban-type settings to safely, humanely and quickly harvest overpopulated whitetails. And they do it with long seasons and liberal limits in areas where firearms are not welcome.

In addition to long, early-opening seasons and liberal bag limits, bowmen also enjoy special hunting privileges. Throughout America, there are many "special hunts" for bowhunters only run by state and federal agencies. Often these hunts are conducted on military bases or properties where firearms hunting is inappropriate. On such land, bowhunter success normally is very high.

In some populated areas, whole counties are off-limits to gun hunting for safety concerns. Yet bowhunting is allowed, and archers score remarkably well.

With so many deer and bowhunting opportunities available, it makes sense to have another new book dedicated to the sport. This one is unique, however, in that it highlights individuals who are experts and innovators in bowhunting whitetails.

In each chapter, one or more hunters describe some of their tactics, techniques and insights. With over 1,000 years of collective experience, harvesting more than 8,000 deer, the thirty-some archers in this book obviously know something about bowhunting for whitetails.

It is my fond hope that the information these sportsmen share will increase the reader's knowledge and appreciation of deer, and bowhunting for these remarkable animals. I'm confident their shared expertise will improve your success afield. But most important, I'm praying that you share this knowledge with friends and family so that all your dawns are bright and cool, every arrow straight and true.

Bob McNally
Switzerland, Florida

About the Author

Bob McNally is one of the most widely read and respected outdoor writers in a field rich with talent. He has hunted throughout much of world over the past 35 years, traveling an average of 50,000 miles annually to pursue game for his stories and photographs.

Bob has been around hunting and the outdoors most of his life. He took his first buck [deer] at age 14, with a bow and arrows given him by legendary bowhunter Fred Bear. He was just 18 when he sold his first outdoor magazine story—to *Sports Afield*.

Bob was born in West Virginia and began his hunting career in Maryland. He grew up in northern Illinois, where hunting is popular and whitetails are king, and attended the University of Wisconsin, where the campus is vacant on opening weekend of deer season.

He has written 11 books and more than 5,000 articles, working for every important outdoor publication in America, including *Field & Stream* and *Outdoor Life*, where he is a member of the writing staff. He has also been a full-time newspaper outdoors editor, hosted a syndicated outdoors show on radio, appeared on many television programs, conducted seminars around the nation—and won more than 150 awards for his writing, broadcasting, and photography.

Bob lives near Jacksonville, Florida, with his wife, Chris, and their children Eric, Matt, and Lindsey.

Bob McNally

PART ONE

GEARING UP

Silence of the Limbs

WITH CUZ STRICKLAND

"Because bowhunting is a close-quarters game, those who are quiet succeed."

T he wind howled and tree limbs swayed, but despite the poor conditions for deer to be on the prowl, suddenly a good buck stepped out of a willow thicket and stood broadside at 15 yards. The eight-pointer's head turned left and right, and his alert twitching nose showed it was time to draw and shoot quickly, before he sensed danger.

Ronnie "Cuz" Strickland didn't have time to check if Tack Robinson had turned on the video camera. His bow came up in the same fluid motion it had a thousand times before. He drew, anchored, and 72 pounds of compound launched an arrow so fast, he never picked up the shaft in flight.

In the swirling wind, Cuz never heard the arrow slam home. But when the deer bolted and ran, he saw the crimson-coated arrow buried in the dirt where the buck had stood.

Cuz turned to Tack, who was in another tree stand, behind him, to see if he'd recorded the action for a Mossy Oak video they were producing. Tack looked at Cuz, shocked and amazed.

"Geezzz! Is that bow quiet!" were his only words.

Cuz smiled but didn't reply, because standing beneath his tree stand was a fat doe. She sniffed at the tree base, and Cuz slowly prepared for a "gimme" shot.

The doe walked out away from the tree and offered an easy 12-yard shot facing away. Cuz drew, anchored, and had his top three sight pins covering the back of her chest, behind the head. He let the arrow go, but incredibly the shaft missed.

"That deer ducked the arrow!" Tack blurted out in disbelief, watching through the video viewfinder.

"No way," Cuz replied. "This bow is too quick and quiet, and that deer was much too close to react fast enough for my arrow to miss. I just made a bad shot. Must have pulled off her somehow."

"Well, I got the whole thing on video, and we'll see what happened," Tack said.

That evening back at their hunting lodge, when Tack played the video, it revealed he was, indeed, correct. In the video, they could hear Cuz's "quiet" bow twang softly, and before the 270-foot-per-second shaft reached the doe, a mere 12 yards away, the deer heard the shot, cringed, and the arrow sailed harmlessly over her back.

Although bowstring silencers can slow arrows down a few feet per second, for whitetail hunting they're a good idea. CREDIT SIMS VIBRATION LABORATORIES

That doe in Tack's video illustrates the importance of making a bow quiet. It proves the fastest bow in the hunting woods can't out-maneuver a deer on alert. Moreover, even a bow tuned so perfectly that it goes off with a mere whisper still can make a deer explode into blurred motion, and send a hunting shaft awry.

The quieter your hunting bow, the more likely you'll be successful with it. And there are some things you can do to "deaden" the sound.

"The first thing a bowhunter should do is understand that he needs a smoother, quieter, and more 'manageable' bow than a 3-D shooter, who wants nothing but bow speed," says Cuz Strickland of Mossy Oak Television Productions, a widely traveled bowhunter with a Boone & Crockett buck to his credit. "Usually, the more arrow speed the noisier the bow, because radical cams store more energy [for speed] than smoother, rounder wheels. Cams vibrate a lot more than round wheels during arrow release."

Cuz advises hunters who want quiet bows to visit a well-stocked archery pro shop and shoot, chronograph, and listen to a number of different bows. One that sounds quiet inside at a pro shop or indoor range will be a whisper when used for hunting in the woods.

"It's usually a good idea to choose a bow that allows the cables or string to set in the longest eccentric wheel slot at a weight that is easily managed by the shooter," Cuz advises. "Bows tend to perform better and quieter when they are long-slotted with the poundage near maximum.

"Bows with one cam are a pretty good compromise, because you get speed with one cam and quiet operation with one wheel."

Cuz says after a bow is selected, proper basic tuning for quiet shooting comes next. He says it's imperative to choose accessories very carefully—rests, overdraws, quivers, and sights contribute to vibration noise—selecting those with as few moving parts as possible. Be certain sight pins, quiver mounts, and overdraws are locked down securely. "Loctite" is an excellent product for securing screws and nuts so they do not become loose yet will "break free" easily, because parts coated with "Loctite" will not rust.

Quivers are some of the most common causes of noise, especially on high-speed bows with radical cams that create a lot of bow recoil. Many hunters have learned the best way to deal with quiver noise is to remove a quiver and hang it in the tree near their stand while hunting. Two-piece model quivers that attach securely to a bow's limb bolts are among the quietest quivers available. "Sims Vibration Laboratory" has many innovative archery products made from the company's remarkable "NAVCOM" material. Its rubber-like "vibration dampeners" of various types can be quickly added to a bow, quiver, and sight to deaden sound. Sims also makes "quiver inserts" of NAVCOM that fit inside a quiver hood to reduce noise and insure broadheads don't rattle or dull from rubbing. Other companies, like New Archery Products (NAP), have similar add-on products.

Quivers are among the most common causes of noise, especially on high-speed bows with radical cams that create a lot of recoil. Archery products made from NAVCOM and "vibration dampeners" of various types can be quickly added to a quiver or other parts to deaden sound.

3

Some bowhunters commonly use thin rubber sheets like gaskets when attaching accessories to absorb and cushion parts during shooting. But Cuz says such gaskets are unnecessary if archers choose simple, well-made accessories.

"A lot of hunters don't take enough time to properly select the right size arrow shaft," Cuz contends. "It's important to use the right shaft size, because if you 'under-spine' arrows, it causes unnecessary vibration."

Sometimes compound bow cables squeak as they pass through a cable slide. A cable slide also can make noise as it moves along a cable guard. Eccentric wheels can become noisy, especially if they're dirty. Even an arrow rest can make a raspy, metallic sound when an arrow is drawn across it. Rubbing all these items with a good non-scent lubricant, such as Vaseline or vegetable oil, helps quiet them. In a hunting emergency, bowstring wax or "Chapstick" can do the trick. Cuz advises using a good grade of special bow lubricant on wheel axles to prevent squeaks. Game Tracker makes a product called "Scent Eliminator Odorless Lubricating Oil" that's superb for silencing moving parts on bows.

Covering the bow shelf and area around an arrow rest with felt or moleskin is a basic and important step in keeping a bow quiet. A felt covering on overdraws near an arrow rest make sense, too. Not only does felt deaden the metallic hit of an arrow against a handle riser, it also serves as a shock absorber during a shot. Noisy bow cable "slap" can be deadened by wrapping moleskin around cables at strategic points where they cross.

Stabilizers are necessary to balance many bows, and while almost any type will do the job, some of the best for hunting are gel- or oil-filled models, or those that use "tuning fork" technology.

Although bowstring silencers can slow arrows down a few feet per second, for whitetail hunting, they're a good idea. They usually work best at dampening vibration when positioned as close to a bow's eccentrics as possible. Many archers prefer rubber string silencers because they don't absorb water, and cockleburs don't stick to them. Sims makes a good one called the "String Leech."

"'Fast-Flight'" string systems on compounds are nice and quiet, because they eliminate the metallic slap of cables," states Cuz. "Many archers use peep sights fitted into their bowstrings. One of the most popular has a one-foot piece of rubber surgical tubing that stretches from the peep sight to the upper bow limb. This long length of tubing makes a loud slapping sound following the shot. To reduce the noise, use a shorter four-inch piece of tubing, and attach it between the peep sight and bow cable."

Some bowhunters have gotten completely away from using peep sights with surgical tubing that can be noisy. They prefer large-hole peeps, and choose models such as the "No Lose Peep" and "Shurz-A-Peep," which turn properly to the eye for a clear sight picture every time the bow is drawn—with no risk of the slapping or breaking problems surgical tubing can cause.

"The first thing I do to make a new, traditional compound bow quiet, is remove the limb bolts while the bow is in a bow press," Cuz explains. "I take the limbs off the handle riser, and on the inside of the 'C-shaped' areas of the riser that holds the limbs, I completely cover them with ultra-thin pool table felt.

"I cut the felt with scissors to fit the entire handle riser ends where the limbs attach, with a hole for the limb bolts to screw back in. The felt acts like a gasket that deadens the shock or thump of a compound bow when it's shot. Next, I take camo tape and completely wrap the limbs where they attach to the riser, which muffles the bow and makes it very quiet."

Cuz says once an arrow leaves a bow, most sound-causing elements have already occurred. But an arrow in flight also can be audible and spook game, especially at long range.

Stand downrange in a safe spot near an archery target (like behind a tree) and listen to arrows as they zip past. Sometimes they whistle in flight from their fletchings, especially feathers, which are noisier than plastic vanes. Sims now has fletches called "Stealth Fletch Vanes," made from vibration-absorbing NAVCOM material, to reduce arrow noise.

A loose broadhead also rattles and makes noise, so be certain broadheads are screwed on tightly.

"A lot of these things may seem pretty nit-picky to some bowhunters," Cuz continues. "But we work so hard, and spend so much time and money to get a shot at a deer, it just makes sense to make a little more effort to ensure your bow is quiet. I know having quiet equipment has definitely produced more deer—especially bucks—for me."

Cuz believes a deer at 20 yards can duck even a super-fast arrow, moving at 300 feet per second, if the animal hears a bow or mechanical release go off.

"One time in Texas, I was videoing a bowhunter using an overdraw bow set at 75 pounds, with a 26-inch 2114 arrow, and a light broadhead," he says. "His bow was shooting an arrow right at 275-feet-per-second. A buck came in and he took a shot at the deer at 18 yards. The animal had its head down and was completely unaware of anything. He shot, and that lightning-fast arrow zipped over the deer's back. We thought he'd just missed the deer, until we viewed the video I'd made of the shot in slow motion. He'd made a perfect, low-chest shot on that buck. But the deer heard the bow's recoil rattle, and dropped straight down at least 16 inches. So the arrow flew over its back.

"Many bowhunters say deer 'jump the string,' or saw the arrow coming and got out of its way. But that's not what happens. A deer hears the bow shot, and instantly cringes to begin its leap away from the unnatural noise. It's like a basketball player who has to bend his knees to jump. A standing deer does the same thing when it's ready to run off. Its first evasive move is to crouch down. So as the deer cringes in preparation to leap, the arrow arrives at the animal and sails over its back. This happens all the time, but I never really knew what occurred until I started watching videos I'd made of bowhunting."

These days, some archers believe their bows are so "fast" that no deer can hear its recoil and move to avoid an arrow. But there is no bow made that can match the reflex actions of a whitetail deer. All bows make "recoil" sounds when they're shot, so experienced hunters go to great efforts to make them as quiet as possible. >

Cuz Strickland, an executive, and on-camera personality with Mossy Oak television, is a highly skilled bowhunter who once owned an archery shop, and has collected countless whitetails from around America. He lives in West Point, MS.

Fast Track to Bow Accuracy

WITH JAY BARRS

"Opening day is just weeks away, but don't panic. You can be ready if you follow these simple archery tips."

Ever notice how bow season sneaks up on you? Sure, you've planted food plots and tended them through summer. You've likely set out trail cameras, even walked the woods a few times checking tracks and sign. You may have spotted a few bucks in a favorite woodlot from long range using binoculars. And perhaps you've even set out a couple of tree stands already in choice spots.

You feel pretty confident, almost smug for the opener. Until—lo and behold—you realize it's only a fortnight away from opening day and your trusty bow from last season has still not been limbered up.

Panic time?

The best thing a beginning or even a rusty bowhunter can do is get some shooting instruction from a professional, and there are a lot of instructors out there, says Olympic gold and silver medalist archer Jay Barrs.

Not to worry. With a little dedication, you'll be on target and ready to "lock-and-load" that bow in no time, thanks in no small part to the fact that modern archery equipment is a marvel of technology. With high-speed compound bows; innovative limb, string, and wheel designs; NASA-inspired vibration dampeners; and arrows, broadheads, rests and sights Fred Bear would find incredible—it's no wonder even a beginning bowhunter can quickly learn to shoot the bulls-eye out of a target at 30 yards.

"The best thing a beginning or even a rusty bowhunter can do is get some shooting instruction from a professional, and there are a lot of instructors out there," says Olympic gold and silver archery medalist Jay Barrs. "A local archery shop or good sporting-goods store is a great place to seek

An anchor point is essential for arrow accuracy, and many bowmen establish two anchor points for even greater consistency.

instruction. There are some videos on the market that are good, too. If those aren't available, then at least try to learn the basics from a friend who's a good archer. Most of them are only too willing to help someone."

Jay says getting "fitted" for proper archery equipment is vital to accurate shooting, much like having the right golf clubs is for a beginning duffer. A bow with proper draw length and draw weight, with matching arrows, is vital to accurate shooting, and a bow pro shop is the place to get fitted.

Many bowhunters have draw lengths that are too long, and they shoot bow weights that are too heavy, Jay believes. For bow poundage, he says an archer should be able to raise his bow in front of him and draw the string straight back without dipping his elbow or straining to bring his arrow to anchor. If he can't draw a bow easily in this fashion, a lesser weight bow should be used. Jay says many noted whitetail hunters commonly shoot bows of only 55 or 60 pounds, and that's plenty adequate for deer. Shooting bows that are too heavy in poundage can be especially difficult for hunters wearing lots of clothing on a cold morning.

Shooting a bow with "an open hand" is important for consistent archery success.

Bowhunters should practice at low bow poundage because it's easier on shoulder joints and muscles. For example, if an archer hunts with a bow set at about 65 pounds, he can reduce bow limb bolts a couple of full turns so he's drawing about 55 pounds during most practice sessions. Bowsights must be adjusted, but it's easier to work on proper shooting technique that produces tight groups with low poundage, says Jay.

Confidence also soars with low bow poundage, and that means a great deal when practice sessions are intense just before hunting season opens. Increase bow weight gradually the last few days before heading to the woods, adjusting sights accordingly. Your muscles will be better tuned, and it's likely you won't need to shoot so many arrows per practice session with heavier bow weight.

Jay says shooting 30 to 40 arrows per practice session, three to four times per week, is ideal in preparation for bow season. But you've got to do it right, starting with the basics.

A proper anchor point is vital to accurate archery, and for bowhunting, an anchor point that's comfortable, quick, and easy to "lock in" is essential. Many different anchor points can be established, with spots on the lips, nose, side of the face, behind an ear, etc., common. Many longtime bowmen have learned to use two anchor points in unison to assure proper hand,

Bowhunters are wise to learn to shoot with both eyes open, not one closed, as most riflemen do.

arm, and head alignment, which leads to consistent bow shooting. Once a proper, comfortable anchor point has been established to create consistency in shooting, Jay says a peep sight and a bowsight should be installed.

A bowman rusty from not shooting during the closed season sometimes forgets to "shoot with a relaxed hand." This simple yet vital part of accurate archery is easy to correct, but not particularly easy to learn if you've not shot this way previously. When a bowman grips a bow's handle tightly, draws, and then releases an arrow, the "shock" or "recoil" from release can cause the bow to torque in the archer's hand. Even the slightest hand torque is enough to kick an arrow out of the sight plane the bowman intended.

To prevent this, at full draw, a bow should not be gripped tightly by an archer. Instead, it should be pulled against the meaty area between the thumb and forefinger of the bow hand. As a bow is drawn, the handle comes to rest in the palm of the hand, with the wrist behind the bow. At full draw, an archer actually "opens his hand," with just the small meaty area between thumb and forefinger supporting the bow.

To prevent torque, an open hand must be kept through a shot. This is difficult for even experienced archers, because once a bowstring is loosed, bow-handle tension against a hand is released and a bow falls. (Gravity, remember?) The experienced bowman instantly grips the bow tightly and prevents it from falling out of his hand. An easier way, explains Jay, is to equip a bow with a wrist sling, which holds it to the archer's wrist through the shot, so he need not worry about dropping his bow while shooting accurately with an "open hand."

A bow sling is simply a leather cord or fabric strap that attaches just below a bow handle; many models secure to a bow's stabilizer connection. A short hunting stabilizer holds the sling in place and aids in accurate shooting. In use, an archer merely slips his hand through the sling, then grips his bow. During a shot, the sling loops around an archer's wrist, behind the bow and arrow rest. At the shot, the bow is allowed to "jump" out of the archer's hand, and the sling prevents it from falling.

Keeping both eyes open when using sights (like a shotgun, not a rifle) is important because it allows the best view of game during a shot. With both eyes open, a bowman can better see the "attitude" of a deer's body, as well as obstructions between hunter and animal that can deflect a shot. Further, in low light, sight pins are easier seen with both eyes open. Having both eyes open may not immediately improve accuracy, but practicing with both eyes open and learning to be comfortable shooting this way, instead of with one eye closed, will result in more successful blood trails.

The old archery adage of "picking a spot" should never be overlooked when tuning up the last couple of weeks before bow deer season, Jay insists. No matter what kind of target you use, you'll shoot tighter groups if you pick as small a "spot" on a target as possible. A small piece of masking tape used as a "spot" on a hay bale, commercial foam target or deer 3-D will help group arrows better. Naturally, keying on a small spot behind a live deer shoulder is critical to accuracy.

Most modern bowhunters use a trigger-type release aid of some type. While such releases are excellent for accuracy, Jay believes too many bowmen use them improperly and are not shooting arrows as accurately as they could.

"A lot of bowhunters 'slap' at their release aid triggers when they shoot, and that's a bad habit," Jay says. "To shoot most accurately, a bow-man must learn to 'squeeze' a release trigger slowly, like a rifleman does. A bow release should almost scare you when it goes off, because you're squeezing it so slowly while aiming."

Jay recommends that at full draw, a bowman habitually first lay his finger on a release-aid trigger, touching it at the first joint of the finger. He says "pulling" with back muscles while slowly squeezing a trigger is the proper way to fire a bowstring release.

"This is not an easy thing to learn, but slowly squeezing and using back tension to trigger a release keeps an archer's head still, and he'll concentrate on his sights and target," Jay says. "When the release goes off, it's really a surprise to the shooter, and a good follow through results."

Proper "follow through" is important in a lot of athletics. The best golfers, baseball, and tennis players follow through with their swings for top results, and it's the same with archery. If you don't "follow through" after you loose an arrow, it won't strike a target precisely where you aim. You can do a lot of crazy things with a bow and arrow during a shot. But if you follow through well, you can still pull off a good hit on a memorable buck.

Proper follow through after a shot isn't hard to master. But if a bow-man hasn't been shooting for long months and quickly tries to get ready for hunting season, he tends to forget this important part of good "form."

The best way to obtain proper follow through is for an archer to hold his bow arm completely outstretched, with his sight never varying from a target, and have his arrow hand in the exact same position through an entire arrow flight, until the shaft strikes home.

Of course, a bowman can't hold his bow arm perfectly still during a shot because of recoil, and his string hand will come back slightly following arrow release. But if a bowhunter tries to make these things occur, he'll have proper follow through and will be well on his way to peak-performance shooting in time for hunting season.

For whitetails, it makes more sense to practice short shots than ones beyond 25 yards, states Jay. The national average for whitetails taken by bow is only 17 yards, which says volumes about the bow-deer game. And while all bowhunters like to practice 40-yard-plus shots, it makes a lot more sense to practice shooting straight down under a tree stand.

"This is one of the most difficult of all bow shots, and one not many hunters practice enough because it seems so easy," reports Jay. "The key to making this shot is to draw a bow while standing upright as you would when shooting at a deer standing at 20 yards. Then, at full draw, bend at the waist, and aim straight down. You'll have to aim a bit low, and the target is usually small [often just the spine area of a deer], but don't overlook practicing it. Don't be satisfied until you can consistently hit a matchbook-size spot."

Finally, Jay says don't forget to have fun when practicing for bowhunting.

"You want to look forward to archery practice, and that's easy to do by setting up balloon or clay targets, or . . . a small competition between a few friends," he says. "When we were training for the Olympics, we'd shoot at 90 meters, and the person who shot the poorest had to walk down the range and get all the arrows for everyone. That was a pretty good incentive for us to shoot well, and it was fun needling the guy who had to make that long walk getting, well, the shafts."

Jay Barrs is a world-class archer. He was a member of the U.S. Olympic archery team in 1988, 1992, and 1996, and has won both Olympic gold and silver medals. Jay is also an enthusiastic bowhunter, with record-book whitetails to his credit. He lives with his wife, Janet, also an Olympic archer, in Salt Lake City, Utah.

Here We Go Loop-de-Loop
WITH PETE SHEPLEY

"Increase accuracy and save string wear with this simple rope trick."

Archers are incurable tinkers. Tighten a screw or nut here. Try a new gizmo there. Use this sight, that stabilizer . . . perhaps get a new quiver or release aid . . . or change the draw length or eccentrics.

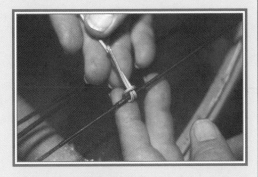

Tie a "reverse half-hitch" knot at the spot where the arrow should be nocked on the bowstring.

All these little custom touches are much of what makes archery and bowhunting fun. The goal is ever-tighter groups, consistent accuracy, better broadhead flight and penetration, quieter and faster bows and, ultimately, more and bigger bucks per season. To reach that end, bow-and-arrow setups are usually very different among archers. There's a lot of pride in such customization, and a bit of competition among bowmen over who has better, newer, faster, or quieter gear.

We all learn from each other. When your pal extols the virtues of a hot broadhead or sight, you listen carefully, perhaps eventually incorporating it into your hunting setup. So when top archer and bowhunter Pete Shepley of PSE Archery talked about rigging string loops on bows, everyone within earshot listened.

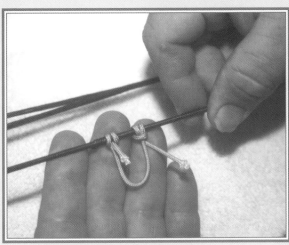

Tying a second reverse half-hitch knot creates the basic "string loop."

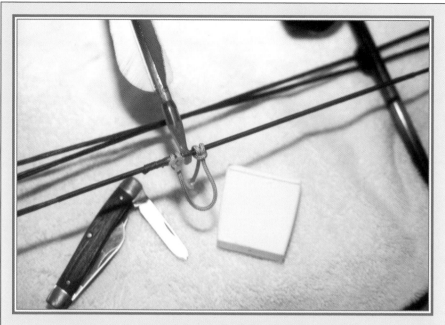

Serve the top reverse half-hitch knot in place with dental floss.

"You'll shoot tighter groups more consistently," he said. "And you'll save wear on a bowstring serving when using a caliper release. Almost all 3-D tournament shooters use loops, and those same shooters wouldn't think of bowhunting without them."

Pete convinced most everyone listening to make the switch to "strip loops," because when a new item of equipment makes it to general use on the 3-D tournament circuit, then starts to flourish among bowhunters in tree stands around the nation, it's time to look very hard at that gear.

The so-called "string loop" or "release rope" is an interesting, innovative, and inexpensive little piece of equipment that has taken target archery and bowhunting by storm. It is simply a small piece of braided nylon cord that's secured to a bowstring just above and below the spot where an arrow is nocked. It's best used with a caliper-style release aid which, according to the archery industry, is by far the most common method of shooting employed today—used by something like 85 percent of all archers.

The primary value of a string loop is that it eliminates upward pressure associated with caliper releases against standard metal nocking points. The upward pressure and severe "pinching" effect at full draw tends to make arrows fly erratically. This is a particular problem with short, fast compound bows that have an especially acute string angle at full draw when shot with a caliper release using only a standard nocking point.

Constant shooting with a caliper release aid wears quickly on a bowstring serving. And reserving a bowstring is time-consuming and can get touchy, since new nocking points must be set, and that usually means the bow must be sighted in again. But string loops eliminate bowstring wear. When one begins to fray, simply cut it off and tie on anoth-

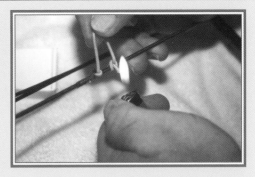

Burn the tag ends of the reverse half hitch knots to secure them.

er. Sighting-in with a new string loop is usually fast, since you can easily mark exactly where to tie it on a bowstring with a felt pen.

Another benefit is that a string loop makes it easy to slightly adjust bow draw length. Just make a larger loop for increased draw length, a smaller loop for less draw length. One plus of a larger-then-usual string loop is that for hunting purposes, it's very fast to attach a caliper release to an oversize loop. Many archers find that a large loop is quiet and performs at least as well as a small string loop.

Setting up a string loop is easy. But for archers who are all-thumbs, save time by asking a friend who knows how to help you, or check with an archery pro shop.

String loop material can be purchased through mail-order catalogs, but it's easy to locate suitable cord locally at archery shops and elsewhere. Some archers use parachute cord or 2 mm nylon cord found in camping supply stores. Others have found that the cord from old Venetian blinds is tough, cheap, and just the right diameter.

The first step in installing a string loop is locating the spot where an arrow should be nocked. This is done as usual, with an arrow placed on the bow rest, then snapped on the bowstring. Slide the arrow to the approximate spot where you believe it should be posi-

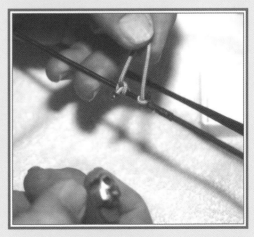

Burning the nylon tag ends creates a melted "ball," which prevents knot slippage. Be sure to coat knot ends with epoxy, too.

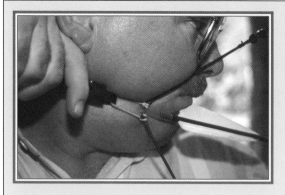

A large string loop eliminates upward pressure associated with caliper releases against standard metal nocking points. This extra-large string loop makes snapping on a release quick and easy, and it quickly increased the bow's draw length.

tioned (usually 1/8-inch above square), and use a felt pen to mark the bowstring above and below the arrow nock.

Remove the arrow and use a "reverse half-hitch" knot to tie one end of the cord to the bowstring, right on the felt pen mark. Using the same-type knot, tie the cord so it covers the other felt pen mark. Keep the knots loose until you determine the length string loop you desire. Nock an arrow and wiggle the half-hitch knots so the arrow nock is snug between the nylon. Then tighten the half-hitch knots using needle-nose pliers, and trim the knots, leaving 1/4-inch tag ends.

Next, with a lighter, burn the tag ends of the reverse half-hitch knots so a "ball" of nylon is produced. This keeps the ends from slipping through the knots. Many archers also dab the nylon ball with a bit of epoxy as further insurance against slipping.

At first you may not believe that a couple of reverse half-hitch knots won't slip, and this really gets your attention as you draw 70 pounds of bow, since a string-loop failure at the wrong moment could result in a busted lip or lost tooth. But rare is the string loop that slips. Now hit the range and shoot a few arrows to get comfortable with the setup.

Paper tuning follows next, and if you learn that the nocking point must be adjusted a tad high or low, spinning the string loop around and along the bowstring serving is a snap. Moving the loop is much easier than removing an old metal nocking point, pinching another one on, then paper tuning again, and again, and again.

In adjusting a string loop up or down, be sure to turn both knots simultaneously, to keep the same gap you set for snug-fitting arrow nocks. Once you've paper tuned so you're satisfied the string loop is perfectly positioned on a bowstring, lock it in place by serving above the top half-hitch knot with dental floss. Some bowmen simply crimp on a metal nock above the top knot to keep the string loop from moving—and it will move if it isn't secured. >

A Bowman's Daypack

WITH JOELLA BATES

"Having needed gear with you in the woods makes for more enjoyable bowhunting, and increases the odds for success."

Rare is the bowhunter who has not spent a less-than-enjoyable time on stand in a deer woods because he forgot his insect repellent, or roll of toilet paper (used for marking a blood trail, too). And many veteran bowhunters have lost count of the times their deer grunt call, compass, flashlight or other important piece of hunting gear was lost or forgotten, just when they needed it most for a day in whitetail country.

"There are no complete assurances that a bowhunter always will have all accessory gear needed for a comfortable hunt. But one of the best moves an archer can make to keep important archery items together is to have a quality backpack used exclusively for bowhunting," says widely traveled and highly respected bowhunter Joella Bates. "My backpack has items added to it and taken out through the course of a season as needs arise or diminish, and at times it's pretty heavy. But most whitetail bowhunters don't walk too far, rarely more than a few hundred yards. And I'd rather have everything I need with me in my pack, and be comfortable, so I can sit in a stand for six or eight hours, or all day if I choose to."

One of the best moves an archer can make to keep his important archery items together is to have a quality backpack used exclusively for bowhunting, says widely traveled and highly respected bowhunter Joella Bates.

17

Joella packs a wealth of equipment into her soft-sided daypack. While heavy, it makes her time in the woods more pleasant, and makes her a more alert, better hunter.

Joella says there are certain essentials that never leave her pack because of the vital role they play in a tree stand. Her SOG multi-tool, with its pliers, knife, screwdriver and other implements is always in her pack. Also, a small super-sharp folding saw and pruning shears are included for trimming branches to make open shooting lanes where deer are expected.

Joella keeps food in her pack for energy—preferring small packages of sunflower seeds, granola bars and fruit—as well as a small pad of paper and pencils for making notes while on stand, or drawing stand locations and spots where buck rubs and scrapes are seen from the treetops.

Other "must-have" pack items for Joella include a quality compass, grunt deer call, doe bleat can call, diaphragm turkey call, folding lock-back knife and knife sharpener (useful for broadheads, too). She also has trail-marking reflective tape and ribbon, toilet paper (placed in a plastic bag to keep it waterproof), a paperback book to help pass the time and a Thermacell insect-repellent unit. In her pack, too, are lighter and matches (sealed in a 35mm film canister), a hand-size portable urinal, powder and "floater" wind-check devices, a full water bottle, and a 30-foot-long pull-up cord.

The cord has clips at each end for easy attachment to a bow and to Joella's belt or tree stand. A couple of screw-in tree steps are necessities, too, even though most of the time Joella hunts from a climbing stand. A tree step can be used to hang a bow or a hunting pack, especially on pine trees, which often lack low branches for hanging gear.

Joella has made it a habit to have two sets of camouflage face masks and gloves, and two sets of arm guards and release aids in her pack. These items are an absolute necessity, and should one become misplaced (common during the confusion of a multi-day hunt), a back-up is immediately at hand. Another plus for carrying two arm guards/release aids and two face masks/gloves is that if she drops one while putting them on up in the treetops, it's not necessary to climb all the way down to the ground to retrieve it.

She uses doe in estrus scent during the rut, and carries it in her pack. She also totes small binoculars, a 35mm camera, a MagLite flashlight and another small flashlight that attaches to her hat for hands-free use. She keeps her full safety harness in her pack, so she can find it quickly when it's time to put it on before climbing a tree. She also stows a "Gibbs Gear" cloth bow sling in her pack, removing it and putting it on her bow for easy over-the-shoulder carrying when walking to and from stands.

In cooler weather, Joella favors fleece clothing—a jacket, hand muff, cap, gloves and neck warmer—most of it "Raven Wear" from Canada. Fleece is warm and quiet, and it repels rain and dew. Sometimes she includes chemical-packet hand warmers in her pack, which keeps her comfortable during a damp dawn. Joella uses a full-size "Critters

Some specialized packs have compartments where a bow can be toted. This is desirable because it allows an archer to have both hands free for doing other important tasks—like dragging out a buster buck.

Dreams" backpack for toting stand-hunting accessories. But some hunters prefer smaller fanny packs, and others simply stuff items into large cargo-pants pockets. A lightweight, fleece-covered "daypack" with large and small two-zipper compartments can be good, as long as the zippers are plastic, rust and jam proof. The fleece makes for quiet pack access. Some good packs also have an exterior draw-string-secured pocket for an easy-to-reach plastic water bottle. When it's cool, a small Thermos of beef broth or coffee can be substituted for water.

Most good packs have a center-top hanging loop so that they hang vertically in a stand, which is important for easy access. The zippered compartments can be left half open (at their tops) so you can reach into them while the pack is hanging on its loop. Rooting around in the pack can be done quickly, quietly and easily, without scraping tree bark or causing so much of a ruckus that deer are alerted.

"One major plus for a stand pack devoted exclusively to bowhunting is you always know what's inside, so it's ready to go when you are," explains Joella. "And carried on your back with padded straps, it's no strain walking even long distances over rugged terrain. I've come to rely on my pack and its ever-ready contents just as much as I depend on a quality bow, arrows, broadheads, tree stands and other important hunting gear." >

Joella Bates *was born and raised in Tennessee, where she started hunting with her father at age six, and took her first deer at age 14. She has a wildlife degree from the University of Tennessee and a masters degree in fisheries management, and at one time she was a Tennessee wildlife officer. Currently, she is a professional tournament archer, and has won five world 3-D championships. Joella has collected more than 50 whitetails with a bow, as well as 48 species of game, including cape buffalo and moose.*

Monster Broadheads

WITH DR. WARREN STRICKLAND

*"Are oversized expandable heads more
lethal than small ones?
Read on to learn more."*

I
t was colder than a witch's heart that daybreak in mid-November
on the Iowa farm. But it was, without question, the best weather for
hunting the bowman had during a week of chasing rutting, barrel-neck
bucks. Finally the wind had died, and the sloppy rain/sleet stopped. It was 11
degrees, so cold and still a bowhunter could almost hear the woods shivering.

The hunter's tree stand was in a gnarly cottonwood, high above a dry
creek, beside a cut soybean field. Several trails through waist-high grass
showed that deer were regularly working out of the cottonwood bottom
and into the beans. At first light, two small bucks slipped along the bean
field edge, one grunting with every step directly under the hunter's stand.

Across the field he watched
another small buck chase a
doe; then a bigger, better buck
chased the small buck away.

Things were looking good,
thought the archer after watching all the sudden buck activity
a bit after the sun was up.

Right then, movement down
in the draw near the dry creek
caught the archer's eye. A heavy
buck with a decent rack was
moving steadily toward him.

The deer crossed the creek,
locked onto a trail leading up
out of the draw, and climbed
toward the rim of cottonwoods
and the bean field. He crossed
an opening at 18 yards and the

Short tracking jobs are the rule with oversize expandable-blade broadheads.

hunter, grunting softly to stop him, came quickly to full draw. The buck froze, looking off to learn where the sound had come from, as the archer touched the release and the carbon shaft flashed into the massive brown body.

The hunter thought the arrow hit the buck a bit too far forward. But the shaft buried to its nock, and the hit sounded like someone smacking an oak tree with a 2x4. The buck turned away, charging down a ridge and launching off the near side of a steep creek bank, where it vanished. It never climbed the far side of the creek. The hunter heard the buck fall heavily, and knew the eight-pointer was down for good.

The entire event, from shot to buck crash, hadn't taken 10 seconds. The bowman was stunned that the deer was down so fast, traveling only 50 yards before he succumbed.

The deer was soon recovered and trucked to a farmhouse. The buck's live weight was well in excess of 250 pounds, as it bottomed-out a farm

Even big bucks fall to big-head expandables. This 172-inch Kansas buck was taken by noted New York archer Ernie Calandrelli using carbon shafts with expandable-blade broadheads and only 60 pounds of bow draw weight.

scale. When the animal was cleaned, the bowman learned just how well his arrow had performed.

The shaft had gone completely through the animal. The hit was a bit forward, but the broadhead had completely blown through both tough shoulder bone plates, leaving holes so large that an entire open hand could pass through them easily.

The carbon shaft had splintered, but the 125-grain, two-blade Game Tracker "Terminator" broadhead had retained its shape well. The two over-size 2¾-inch-long blades were nicked profusely, and one blade was bent beyond re-use, but the broadhead tip and ferrule were undamaged.

Right then the archer decided that oversize or "monster" expand-able-blade broadheads were something very special in putting down white-tails in a hurry. He began analyzing the deer he'd taken with such heads, and made very careful note of the whitetails that followed.

That heavyweight Iowa buck was one of over 30 whitetails the archer took with "monster" expandable heads—larger than two inches in diameter. The hunter either saw every one of those deer fall while watching from his tree stand, or heard them go down heavily in very thick, tangled vegetation. The farthest any of those animals ran was 75 yards. Most succumbed within 50 yards; many took but a hop or two before toppling. Not a single deer had been lost. Not one.

It was enough to convince the hunter that there was no better hunt-ing setup for whitetail deer than carbon arrows, and oversize, expand-able-blade broadheads.

Such a preference for giant, wide-cutting broadheads requires that the head have expandable or "mechanical" blades. This is simply because a broadhead with a two-inch or wider cut can't be shot as accurately as a low-profile expandable that has virtually no wind resistance. Indeed, it's the reason so many modern whitetail bowhunters prefer expandable broad-heads. They fly almost like field points, with much more accuracy than ever can be attained with any of even the best fixed-blade designs.

"I'm a firm believer in expandable-blade broadheads, and I also believe the bigger the head, the more tissue damage that results, and the faster an animal goes down," says Unionville, Alabama, cardiologist Dr. Warren Strickland, with over 100 big-game animals to his archery credit using expandable broadheads. "There is a big difference in how much hemorrhag-ing, how much blood loss there is, and how much resulting shock to an ani-mal is produced—comparing a broadhead with a 1¼-inch diameter cut, and another head with a two-inch cut. When you start comparing a 2¾-inch cut head to one half that size, the difference is incredible, absolutely astounding.

"Another way to look at this is comparing on deer the effects of a .243 caliber bullet and a .300 magnum bullet. Hit a buck with the .243 and he goes down. Hit that buck in the same place with a .300 and he goes down much faster. It's the same with a broadhead.

"Using a very large broadhead is especially important with a bad hit on game. The larger head is going to increase the odds of recovering that animal at least 100 percent because it's going to produce much more bleeding due to the size of the cutting surface, and the size of the holes it produces."

Dr. Strickland uses three-blade mechanical heads with a two-inch diameter cut. He favors such heads having solid aluminum ferrules, which he believes aids in energy retention to facilitate penetration. With it, he recently shot a huge moose, which ran only 70 yards before falling.

"I think a 'trocar' or pyramid-style tip on expandable broadheads is important, too, because it helps a head split bone," explains Dr. Strickland,

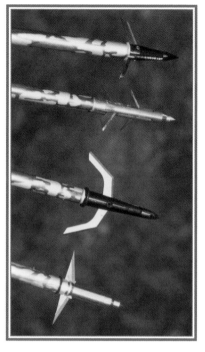

Oversize or "monster" expandable-blade broadheads are something very special in putting down whitetails in a hurry.

whose professional training has given him a thorough understanding of the inner workings of animals, blood supply and trauma.

"Big three-blade expandables used with carbon shafts, and shot with at least 65 pounds of kinetic energy, are absolutely deadly on deer," says Dr. Strickland. "You can probably get away with slightly less pounds using two-blade heads, maybe 60 pounds. Lighter than that, the size head should probably be reduced to help penetration, like no more than a two-inch, two-blade head with 50 pounds of bow draw weight." >

Dr. Warren Strickland, an archer who has traveled the world, hails from Alabama, where he can bow-hunt deer for more than four months every year. He has taken many whitetails with bow and arrows, and avidly hunts them fall through winter.

When a Broadhead Hits

"Razor-edged broadheads are deadly on deer.
But what's the survival rate of animals
not recovered by bowmen?"

T he incredible resiliency of the whitetail deer is something nearly every hunter underestimates, according to Dr. Randy Davidson, professor for the Southeastern Cooperative Wildlife Disease Study (SCWDS) program at the University of Georgia's College of Veterinary Medicine in Athens.

The SCWDS works with the wildlife agencies of 15 Southeastern states and the U.S. Fish and Wildlife Service to study diseases in wild game throughout the Southeast. During the course of such study over the years, the SCWDS has inspected many whitetail deer that have survived remarkable injuries, some inflected by hunters. That some of these

The resiliency of the whitetail deer is something nearly every hunter has experienced. Deer are capable of recovering from injuries that would quickly kill other animals.

animals survive at all is mindboggling, but many apparently thrive and lead comparatively normal wild lives even after such injuries.

"I once inspected a four-and-a-half-year-old doe that had been wounded by an arrow one fall, and shot and killed the following year in Arkansas' very tightly controlled Pine Bluff Arsenal," says Davidson. "I was doing a whitetail disease study on the area and inspecting deer shot during a special hunt that year to determine their health. The hunt manager knew a bowman the previous year had shot and 'lost' a big doe. That four-and-a-half-year-

Whitetails often live with debilitating injuries, and survive very well. This broken back foot belonged to a 175-inch, six-and-a-half-year-old buck that was taken by a bowman as the deer chased does during the rut.

old animal, after having been severely wounded, had bred and had a fawn the following year.

"There was no doubt it was the same doe that had been 'lost' by the bowman the previous year. The deer still had six inches of arrow shaft and a broadhead embedded in it.

The arrow had penetrated from the top of the animal near the rear right leg. It went forward through the diaphragm, penetrated the chest cavity, and into the thorax. There was some inflammation around the wound, but the arrow shaft was completely encapsulated in scar tissue and the doe didn't seem to have had any ill effects from the wound whatsoever. Otherwise she should not have come into estrus, mated, and had young."

Such descriptions of animal wounds sound horribly gruesome to non-hunters. But because true archery sportsmen strive for swift, clean

Author Bob McNally arrowed this heavy-beam, 164-inch Missouri buck using a 70-pound bow, carbon shafts, and a 2.75-inch wide, two-blade expandable broadhead. The buck ran only 35 yards before falling.

kills of all game, learning about the recuperative capabilities of deer is intriguing, since during the course of most hunters' careers, sooner or later they wound an animal, or one of their companions does. Under such circumstances, the discussion around the hunt camp invariably is whether or not the injured animal survived the shot.

Most hunters, especially bowmen, have long believed that an arrow shaft penetrating the diaphragm or thorax causes mortal wounds to deer. But Davidson's inspection of the Pine Bluff Arsenal doe suggests otherwise. This is good, important news to many archers, who commonly are distraught after they shoot and hit a deer with an arrow, yet fail to find it after trailing the animal for hundreds of yards.

Many experienced bowhunters believe a well-shot deer not found dead after properly trailing the animal for about 500 yards recovers from a broadhead wound. This theory assumes that during the course of trailing, an animal is never "jumped," since a wounded whitetail roused from its bed can travel great distances before succumbing. So any deer arrow shot in a spot other than the chest should be given long hours before tracking.

Davidson, who hunts deer with bow and rifle, does not agree totally with the 500-yard distance theory, but he comes close.

"The 500-yard distance theory of some bowhunters is probably correct, but I'd hate to state that yardage as gospel," he declares. "However, I'd

Many experienced bowhunters believe that a well-shot deer not found dead after properly trailing it for about 500 yards will recover from a broadhead wound.

say a large portion of deer that are shot but not found by a bowhunter, do survive. That's my opinion, based on my observation and studies of many animals that have had obvious archery wounds prior to the ultimate cause of their demise and my inspection of the animal. Some of these injuries are very dramatic, yet the animals are alive and seem to be doing okay. Thus when many bowhunters make what they believe are fatal shots on deer—if the animal is not found—they are mistaken, and the deer does not die.

"The concept of a deer laying around for weeks suffering from an arrow injury is not correct in most situations. Most arrow-wounded animals die within a very short time, or they recover—though sometimes with some type of a detectable problem."

Many contemporary wildlife researchers report that a modern arrow striking vital deer parts kills very quickly, within seconds, and rarely does an animal live more than a minute. Deer hit in non-lethal spots may bleed profusely for a short time. Then, because the cut is quick and clean, bleeding stops and, much of the time, the deer survives. It's much like a shaving cut with a new razor blade—lots of blood at first, but the wound soon seals and heals.

Davidson once inspected a deer—killed by other means—that had a broadhead and one inch of arrow shaft embedded in its cranium. Yet the deer was healthy and had recovered from that arrow wound before later being shot and killed by another hunter. Incredibly, this situation is not unique.

In 1986, a Wisconsin firearms deer hunter shot a young buck that had a broadhead imbedded nearly one inch into its brain. Badger State game officials checked the deer and believed it was shot as a button buck the previous season, and lived to 18 months of age while carrying the broadhead. Skull bone tissue had encapsulated the arrow and broadhead, and the young buck had been living what was believed to be an ordinary life.

Another remarkable, well-documented case of a buck surviving seemingly mortal wounds occurred in 1988 at the Squaw Creek National Wildlife Refuge in north Missouri. Veteran archer Curtis Taylor collected a P&Y record buck with a 127⅞-inch rack. On closer inspection, the deer also toted two other broadheads, four lead slugs and a number of shotgun pellets. Yet the 205-pound buck seemed to have weathered the arsenal of hunter projectiles well until Taylor collected the trophy.

Davidson has seen whitetails that survived after having pieces of their spines and lungs shot away. Even more impressive to him is the whitetail's ability to survive severe leg injuries. He has inspected deer that were hit by automobiles, rifle bullets, shotgun pellets and broadhead arrows. Some animals have had legs completely cut off, compound leg fractures and broken ribs, yet they still survived. Often the fractures mended with misaligned bones, but the deer seemed to do quite well in the wild.

Today's archer is much more efficient than yesterday's hunter.

Davidson and his biology crew once inspected a doe that had a perfect broadhead "X" through the chest cavity in the high lung area. The shot looked to be perfect, but no damage had been done to the lungs. Apparently at the exact instant of arrow impact, the deer had just completely exhaled, deflating its lungs. Thus the shaft zipped through the deer without mortally wounding it, no doubt baffling the archer who had made what he surely believed was a killing shot.

It's instances such as these that leave many bowhunters dumbfounded and disheartened when the blood trail they believe is short leads to no downed game. Such tales also can leave listeners believing bowhunters kill and lose many more deer than they do.

For example, a paunch- or stomach-shot deer is the ultimate horror of every hunter, because almost all sportsmen believe an animal shot there will die slowly. Moreover, most hunters believe the paunch wound is always fatal to deer because infection is inevitable. Davidson, however, says otherwise—at least when arrows and broadheads are involved.

"Frankly, if I were a deer, that's one place [the paunch] where I'd pick to be hit by an arrow," Davidson explains. "There is no question some deer shot in the paunch survive, probably a lot more than most hunters ever dream possible—especially from an arrow wound which is so clean. The biological reason for this is pretty simple: Deer, like cows and sheep, have evolved a protective outer lining around the paunch that helps plug small holes that naturally poke through intestines because of the rough, sharp forage the animals eat, like briers, straw, twigs, browse, etc. This lining is a fibrous, net-like, lacy substance that looks like cheesecloth and covers most of the abdominal viscera. Its purpose is to plug holes poked in the wall of the intestine—which is precisely what it does with the wound generated by a bowhunter."

Unlike shotgun pellets or arrow wounds, Davidson has seen very few deer survive a high-powered rifle bullet to the body. He has inspected deer that lived following rifle bullet wounds to their extremities, but the fatality rate of animals hit in the body by a rifle projectile is extremely high, he says. This may be one reason why some people's perception of bowhunters is that they cripple many deer, since those shot with an arrow in the body that doesn't pierce a major organ may heal, survive, and so are never found, while a rifle-shot deer struck in the same place will die, though it may not be recovered by the hunter until much later. When another hunter harvests the arrow-hit deer and the broadhead wound is discovered, some people mistakenly believe many deer are shot by bowmen, but die later without recovery.

Dr. Ward Stone is with the New York State Department of Environmental Conservation Wildlife Pathology Unit. He has examined thousands of deer to determine the cause of death.

"Protracted morbidity caused by arrow wounds, resulting in death of deer, is rare," he says. "I have seen only two cases involving arrow wounds of the head that resulted in the death of the deer. In my experience as a wildlife pathologist, the arrows used today by deer hunters generally cause

Many contemporary wildlife researchers report that a modern broadhead arrow striking vital deer parts kills very quickly, within seconds, and rarely does an animal live more than a minute.

quick kills. Wounds caused by arrows that are not immediately fatal generally heal more swiftly than bullet wounds. This is in part due to the less tissue destruction resulting from the incised wounds caused by arrows."

For over 20 years, "Deer Search," a New York deer-hunting organization, has used leashed tracking dogs to recover wounded game, both gun- and archery-shot animals. Hunters who have shot deer and can't find them contact the group, which then tracks the animals using the trained dogs. Dr. John Jeanneney founded the organization, and says that arrow-shot deer are more difficult for tracking dogs to recover than gunshot animals.

"Although conclusive proof is lacking, I strongly suspect that a bow-hunter tends to wound more deer than a gun hunter. But the mortality rate from these (bow) wounds is considerably lower. A broadhead can narrowly miss a major blood vessel, and yet make a clean wound that bleeds for only a short time and heals without infection. Rifle bullets and shotgun slugs smash bone and drive hair into the wound, often producing gangrene even when vital organs are not involved."

African animals are not whitetail deer, of course. But an extensive study conducted by Tony Tomkinson (bowman and chief ranger at the Mkuzi Game Reserve in the Republic of South Africa) is interesting in showing how effective broadheads are, compared to bullets. During 1985, of 96 big-game animals harvested, he learned the wounding rate by bow-men was significantly higher than for rifle hunters. But he noted that animals mortally wounded by arrows traveled less than 30 yards farther than similar animals shot with a .30-06 rifle.

Tomkinson's study suggests that while archers hit and lose more big-game animals than firearm hunters, game struck in non-lethal areas by an arrow survives very well. A rifle bullet hitting the same non-lethal spot does so much tissue and bone damage, that animal's death is almost assured, though protracted.

Survivability of deer from non-fatal arrow wounds is at the crux of this discourse. But much of the scientific data gathered about bowhunting deer is comparatively "old," at least for a sport like archery that has advanced so much in such a short time. The bows, arrows, broadheads, sights, release aids, and other equipment used just a decade ago seem like Neanderthal gear now. Today's archer is far more efficient than yesterday's hunter. He is much more capable of putting a broadhead arrow through the vital area of a whitetail buck at 20 yards than he was just 10 years ago. And that arrow, placed where aimed, is nearly as deadly on game as a bullet. If the shaft misses its mark, odds are good the animal will survive.

"My perception is that gun hunters who complain about bowhunt-ers crippling game is that they [gun hunters] don't have any first-hand experience of finding deer mortally wounded by an arrow," explains Davidson. "Their [gun hunters'] opinion is based solely on being at the local sporting-goods store and hearing a bowhunter say he hit a deer and didn't recover it. Most likely, the arrow-shot animal did survive, but a gun hunter overhearing the conversation doesn't think so because he can't conceive of an animal surviving a hit from a .30-06. He has no idea what a modern broadhead arrow does to game." >

PART TWO

GETTING READY

Small-Tract Deer Management

WITH JIM CRUMLEY

"You don't need thousands of acres for great bow deer hunting."

I t was the last day of the late-phase Virginia archery season and Tom Smith needed a deer for his freezer. The land he hunted was a 200-acre tract owned by his brother-in-law, Jim Crumley of Trebark Camouflage. Tom went to a familiar tree stand late that afternoon, a place he was almost certain he'd see deer within bow range, resulting in choice steaks for a long, Virginia winter.

But that night, back at the Crumley home, Tom was noticeably grouchy because he hadn't shot a deer.

"I can't believe it; I'd have bet I'd arrow a deer from that stand," he complained.

"That is strange," said Jim as he consoled his brother-in-law. "I saw a lot of deer from my stand, and I could have arrowed a number of big does. I wanted a buck, though, one eight-points or better, in keeping with the harvest restrictions we have on this property. You didn't see any deer from your stand?"

The question changed the expression on Tom's face noticeably.

"Well, yes, I saw deer," he replied, now beginning to smile. "In fact, I saw seven deer, but all of them were bucks. There were several spikes, a six-pointer, and a couple of forkhorns . . . but no does! Cheez! When you want a doe, you just can't seem to find one. Of course, just five years ago I wouldn't have seen any deer from that stand."

Indeed, Jim had changed his 200-acre homestead hunting spot from an area nearly devoid of deer into a veritable whitetail Mecca. And he did it with just a bit of common sense, sound game management, and the proper planting and cultivation of food plots and native deer browse.

"When I bought my place five years ago, I could walk the entire property and not jump a bedded deer," Jim explains. "Today, I couldn't walk an hour—at any time of day, any season of the year—without jumping deer. What we've done here isn't something magical, and it doesn't take a lot of money. It used to be a rule of deer management that you needed at least 500 acres to have any effect on animals. But most biologists say that isn't

Jim Crumley says one important way to quickly make a small tract into a good bowhunting spot is to allow no gun hunting on the property. He also suggests restricting the bucks harvested; eight points or better is a good rule.

so today. In fact, I'm convinced a person could take as little as 50 acres and, if the surrounding land isn't ravaged by other hunters, manage that 50 acres well enough that he'd have good archery deer hunting for himself and his family.

"I started managing land for bowhunting deer when I had just 66 acres. In just a few years we made it into a heck of a good spot, where we shot a number of whitetails every year with bows and arrows. Then I bought my new place, and in five years we really made a difference in deer numbers and the quality of animals on my 200 acres."

The first season that Jim hunted his 200 acres, he was lucky to see an eight-point buck, and during the first four years, he never saw a buck with a rack scoring more than 125 Pope & Young points. But in the fifth year of managing the land, he saw three different bucks that would score over 125 P&Y points each, and the land is now alive with lesser bucks and plenty of mature does.

How did he do it? What's his secret for success?

"First, I've allowed no gun hunting on the property," he explains. "Also, we have a strict rule that no bucks less than eight points can be shot, even by archers. Mature does are fine, but we preserve the bigger bucks. In five seasons, we only took five bucks with racks eight points or better.

The most important land management Crumley has done to his small tract of property is planting food plots. Some are very small, just 20 yards by 40 yards.

Crumley says a good perennial rye grass food plot is actually more important to deer than white oaks, because it produces more food, more consistently.

"Naturally, we've also managed the land to make it more nutritionally desirable for deer, but it's nothing magical, really. In fact, it's something anyone can do if his property is in even a marginally decent whitetail area. We just provide whitetails good food, shelter and a chance to mature."

The most important land-management action Jim has taken is planting food plots on his property. Some are very small, just 20 yards by 40 yards. But he has one 45-acre fallow field planted in strips. In the larger field, he has perennial rye grass, fertilized blackberry patches and islands of cedar trees (which he says are important winter food for whitetails in Virginia).

"This will sound crazy to some hunters, but a good perennial rye grass food plot is actually more important to deer than white oaks," Jim says. "In some cases, we have pushed over oaks on ridge tops to make food plots planted in rye. White oaks are wonderful deer food. But even in a prime area, white oaks only have good mast acorns once every three years, and they last only a couple of months. In a food plot planted in rye or clover, the nutrition deer receive is for much longer duration, and they get it every year, not just a couple of months every three years."

Jim plants clover in some food plots and he's experimented with alfalfa. But perennial rye is far and away the best crop he's found for whitetails. It doesn't have to be planted every year, and it can be grazed heavily without being killed by the animals. It's also tolerant of heat and cold, so can be planted successfully in many regions. All Jim does to his rye patches is fertilize them once per year and, occasionally, add lime to the soil.

"Deer and turkeys love rye grass, and they get a lot of nutrition from it during times of year they really need it," Jim continues. "Other plants are good in food plots, too, like wheat and partridge peas. But perennial rye is the best because it's available when deer need it most. It comes up in spring when there are no acorns and not much browse, so deer and turkeys really hit it hard. It goes to seed, then turns brown in summer, but deer don't need it then because so much other food is available in the woods. It can be bush-hogged and fertilized, and by fall it comes back strong. It looks so good in autumn that it's like a manicured football field. Deer love and devour it."

Jim cuts bush-hog trails into the woods from food plots. He says deer use the trails so heavily that bowhunting over such places is as close to a sure thing in arrowing a deer as anything he know, short of using bait.

In addition to deer and turkeys, simple land management like food plots also helps quail, rabbit and dove populations. Canada geese can be harvested in lush fields of clover, too.

Jim also manages wild foods on his 200 acres. He broadcasts 10-10-10 fertilizer on blackberry plants, honeysuckle, oaks, persimmons and wild apples. Just a bit of fertilizer can lead to bumper crops of such plants, which are relished by whitetails, and make for outstanding bowhunting spots.

Bowmen should resist the temptation to arrow young bucks for good small-tract management. Wait until they are mature before harvesting them.

Even trails in the woods can be easily planted with a clover blend that grows well in the shade. CREDIT FIDUCCIA ENTERPRISES.

"This kind of small-tract management really works, and it's a lot of fun, too," Jim says, smiling with satisfaction. "It's great to work the land with your own hands and watch game respond positively to the things you do. Best of all, though, you don't have to be a land baron to make a difference with wildlife. It's also nice to be able to reap the rewards of your efforts by knowing you have a pretty good chance of seeing deer every time you're in the woods, and of eventually taking a nice buck that you've grown right on your property." >

Virginia bowhunter Jim Crumley started the modern camouflage craze when he designed Trebark camo. He spends every moment possible in the woods, where he annually takes plenty of whitetails with his bow.

Plotting for Bucks

WITH DR. GRANT WOODS

"Whether you want to attract deer for bowhunting, or grow bigger, healthier animals, you can do it best with food plots."

You know deer love agriculture crops, which is one reason the nation's whitetail population is bursting at the seams. Corn-, bean- and clover-fed bucks are collected by uncountable thousands of hunters nationwide. And for decades, bowhunters have been sowing winter wheat and rye for deer feed, which is why more than one wall-hanger whitetail has been taken from such spots.

But your favorite hunting haunts are different, right? You hunt tangled creek bottoms where big bucks roam. And during the rut, the wooded ridges

Doing it correctly, with proper liming, fertilizing, seed planting, and weed control, sportsmen can produce 5,000 to 10,000 pounds of digestible deer forage per food-plot acre per year—at a cost of between $150 to $300 per acre, explains Grant. CREDIT BIOLOGIC

41

on your property are covered with scrapes and rubs. That hunting hideaway has all the browse, white oaks, red oaks and crabapple trees any whitetail could possibly want to grow a big, healthy, world-class rack, right?

Besides, on good deer land, why go to all the farming effort to "plant" crops, since Mother Nature does such a good job?

"Doing it correctly, with proper liming, fertilizing, seed planting and weed control, I can produce 5,000 to 10,000 pounds of digestible deer forage per food-plot acre per year—at a cost of between $150 to $300 per acre," says biologist and deer/land management specialist Dr. Grant Woods. "The average hardwoods acre grows 50 to 500 pounds of natural deer forage annually, including choice acorns from oaks.

"Thus a well-managed food plot will provide deer, and other game, 10 to 200 times more forage than wild woods can. Man can grow more quality deer food in a one-acre plot than 50 acres of hardwoods can naturally produce. And a food plot does it consistently, year after year, whereas Mother Nature's hardwoods are fickle. Woods can have years with fair-to-poor wildlife forage production, depending on rain, weather and other factors. But man-made, managed wildlife food plots provide deer with nutritional forage almost year-round, depending on their geographic location, while native hardwoods typically have many lean months where forage production is virtually nonexistent."

Woods makes the case for food plots by citing a 2,000-acre hunt property that had poor-quality deer, which he helped manage in the Adirondack Mountains region of New York. One year, seven different food plots totaling 13 acres were planted. The results were astounding: Deer body weights on the property increased by a remarkable 14 percent.

"This no doubt helped the property's overall fawn survival rate, too, and we saw a marked improvement in antler development in subsequent years because it takes two years for racks to noticeably improve after an infusion of higher-nutrition foods grown in plots," Grant explains. "We planted BioLogic [a New Zealand deer food distributed by Mossy Oak] which has about 34 percent protein, and that's why body weights on those deer increased so tremendously. It's important to note that such a significant increase is partly to do with the initial poor health of those New York deer before we planted fields. But there's little question that food plots provide deer with needed nutrition, which often is lacking in plants they normally rely on for sustenance."

Some bowmen complain that while they "manage" for better deer and bigger bucks on their small hunt properties, neighboring landowners don't. The rub is, why should a hunter with food plots and the desire to have better bucks "grow" deer only to have a neighbor shoot the animals if they wander next door?

"That can be a problem," Grant states. "But if you have choice food plots on your 100 acres, deer will spend the majority of their time on and near those fields—not on your neighbor's property. This is advantageous for attracting and holding better bucks, and also in keeping smaller animals on your land, where you'll allow them to grow, instead of wandering over the property line where they could be shot."

In discussing food plots for deer, it's important at the outset to determine your intent. Are plots made simply to attract deer for hunting, or are they established as year-round feeding sites intended to increase overall herd quality? Year-round plots do the most good for does, fawns and buck racks,

Quality deer management is more than just feeding deer during hunting season. Deer need high-quality food 12 months a year—something in the neighborhood of 16 to 20 percent protein. This is what's required to significantly increase deer body weight and antler development. It can be accomplished by creating food.

but there's more work involved. If you're only interested in feeding deer in autumn for hunting, less farm labor is mandated, but you're not influencing the herd health as much as year-round food will.

"Quality deer management is more than just feeding deer during hunting season," explains Grant. "Deer need a high-quality food source 12 months per year, something in the neighborhood of 16 to 20 percent protein. This is what's required to significantly increase deer body weight and antler development. It can be accomplished by feeding high-protein feeds through game feeders, by creating food plots offering deer spring and summer crops, and by fertilizing natural food sources."

Before getting into the food-plot business, it's smart to carefully analyze potential sites on your hunt property, Grant advises. If possible, pick a spot that's close to a deer bedding area, like a swamp or creek bottom. Make sure prominent wind direction is favorable for hunting, regarding the routes deer should use between bedding areas and the plot. Consider, too, where stands or shooting houses will be located to "cover" plots, and the paths hunters use to access stands. Ideally, wind will be in a hunter's face on stand, and his path to a stand will not be crossed by deer coming to the plot.

It's extremely important to pick a spot for creating a food plot that's conducive to growing plants. The area should be dry, with no flooding or prolonged moisture. An ideal spot has loamy surface soil with a clay base 15 to 20 inches down. This type of soil drains quickly from rain, but "holds" good moisture content well below the surface. A potential food-plot site should receive direct sunlight through at least 50 percent of the day. Not enough sunlight reaching a food plot is one of the biggest reasons for crop failure on small hunting sites.

In hilly country, food plots should be planted in bottomland, but not in a flood plain. Further, a northeast slope is a good place for a summer food plot because soil moisture doesn't bake out from the sun. Conversely, for a winter plot, a southwest slope is good because that area receives more sun for longer periods, which is helpful in the shorter, cooler growing season.

In determining whether to have summer or winter food plots, or both, remember that maximum summer nutrition is what grows antlers, and healthy fawns from rich doe milk produces prime whitetail herds. Winter food plots maintain quality animals, too, but more importantly, draw them into the open where they've vulnerable to hunters.

In some heavily forested regions, trees must be cut down and cleared for food plots. On much hunt property, however, cleared areas already exist. The edges of clear-cuts by timber companies are ideal for planting "green strips." Even better are power and gas pipelines. Old, wide logging roads and firebreaks can also be used for planting. Woods lanes and firebreaks, however, can have too much timber canopy that reduces sunlight and limits potential for lush, maximum-producing, whitetail-drawing plants. Also, woods roads usually have very acidic soil from decaying plant matter, so they require additional liming and fertilizing.

If you're going to create your own food plot in the woods, and you've found the best location for it, take time to design the perfect site for hunting. Grant likes irregularly shaped plots, with lots of winding "edge-cover" adjacent to woodlands, but with no "blind-spots" like extended points of timber or pockets in the woods, where a buck could stand out of sight of a hunter on stand. Grant also prefers bowhunting plots no longer than 100 yards, so ranges are most acceptable to archers.

Some sportsmen like long, narrow plots just 20 or 30 yards wide because they tend to make bucks feel safe by not being too far from timber cover. Some hunters cut long, narrow food plots shaped like a "V" or "L," and place stands where the two lines of the "V" or the "L" join. For bowhunters, such shaped food plots are good, but keep them small, so deer stepping out into cultivation are well within arrow range.

On bigger food plots, sometimes leaving a large oak tree or two in the middle of a field makes sense for stand placement. Oaks in such spots also tend to produce lots of acorns from fertilizing and liming, and can be outstanding archery stands. Sometimes, having a wide lane or two leading to the field creates a natural travel path for deer coming to the site—a choice ambush setup for bowmen.

Some sportsmen who like to stillhunt design special "S" or snake-shaped woods lanes as food plots. They plant lanes for hundreds of yards, and during the season they slip-hunt into the wind, hiding behind turns and dips in the lane to spot bucks around the next bend or behind a slight rise in the terrain. Property that has long, winding woods roads or old logging lanes can be easily made into such prime stillhunt food plots. Hunters in some premier whitetail states like Wisconsin, Minnesota and Michigan create miles of food plots on public, county-owned forests. They till, fertilize and seed old logging roads from ATVs, then bowhunt select spots during the open season.

Biologist and deer/land management specialist Dr. Grant Woods likes irregularly shaped plots, with lots of winding "edge cover" adjacent to woodlands. He also prefers bowhunting plots no longer than 100 yards, so ranges are most acceptable to archers. CREDIT BIOLOGIC

Once the location, size and configuration of a deer food plot has been determined, the on-site dirt work begins.

The first step is to get a soil sample of the site, something few hunters want to do, but is without question the surest, quickest, least expensive and most painless way to produce a top-quality food plot. The best way to test soil is to get one shovel full of dirt from six different places in the plot and dump them in a bucket. Mix the dirt thoroughly, take out one pint, and that's the soil sample. Mark carefully on the container which plot on your land the soil was taken from, since different plots may have different soil make-ups.

The soil sample(s) is sent to a Soil Conservation Service, an agricultural university, or to the Whitetail Institute for analysis, which costs a few dollars. Grant says it's important to tell the people analyzing your soil what type of crop you want to plant—a small grain such as wheat, rye or oats, or a legume like clover or alfalfa. If you want to plant BioLogic, says Grant, tell them you want to plant broccoli, which apparently has the same soil requirements. If you don't know what to plant, give the soil analyzers several crop choices, then pick one later.

Soil-test results reveal how much lime the plot requires, and how much and at what ratio elements in the fertilizer are needed for optimum results for the crop you intend planting. Grant strongly advises having custom fertilizer blended for each plot. Most large feed stores offer this service, and while it costs a bit more for a custom-blended fertilizer, the results are excellent and it actually costs less in the long run, he says, because it produces a peak crop yield.

Proper plot preparation is extremely important, with vigorous disking, plowing and tilling to ready the soil. Grant recommends adding only half the recommended fertilizer and lime during the initial disking. He says it's best to put the remaining fertilizer down 30 days later. Disking fertilizer well down into soil prior to seeding helps plant roots go deep as they seek the rich food.

Careful, correct site preparation also makes for the best weed control on plots. A plot should be tilled and disked several times, over several weeks, before seeding. And it shouldn't be tilled more than three inches deep.

One disadvantage of tilling and disking a plot several times prior to planting is that it can make the soil dry. Timing a planting when rain is slated for the area is important to give seedlings a jumpstart. Plant seeds during a drought or a deluge, and you can kiss the whole food plot operation good-bye.

If all this fieldwork sounds a little too involved or too laborious, stop and think how hard you hunt for good bucks now. Moreover, a lot of food-plot drudgery is only during the initial stages of establishing plots and carving them out of the woods. Soil samples, disking, seeding, etc. can be tough work. But for thousands of bowmen, it's a labor of love—something they do in the off-season to bring bucks in their sights during hunting season.

Dr. Grant Woods, of Reeds Spring, Missouri, is a renowned expert on food plots for whitetail deer, with a PhD in wildlife biology, specializing in whitetail scrape and rub behavior. He is a dedicated bowhunter, who has traveled extensively chasing whitetails. He has numerous bow bucks to his credit, including two Pope & Young trophies.

10 Steps to Food Plot Success

1) Select the site carefully. The plot should be in a good whitetail area, where animals are not afraid to visit day or night.

2) The site should have good soil, not rocks, and be well exposed to sun for proper crop growth.

3) Experts say food plots at least a quarter- to one-half acre in size are needed to truly benefit deer. On 200 acres, four to eight such plots are good. Having a number of small plots is beneficial, as bowhunting pressure is spread out.

4) Irregularly shaped food plots often attract deer best. An old, unused logging road is a good choice for a food plot if it meanders through woods, particularly on a ridge top where it's exposed to sun, and drains well.

5) Proper soil preparation is important. Till the ground with a plow or harrow, either by hand or with an ATV.

6) Test the soil by taking a sample of food-plot earth to a county agricultural agent or to a local college. They'll recommend the right amounts of lime and fertilizer.

7) Learn what types of plants work best for your soil and area of the country. What grows well in Texas isn't necessarily what works in Pennsylvania or Wisconsin.

8) Food plots for deer are best when used year-round by animals. Plant suitable crops in spring and fall, so deer get the most nutrition from the site.

9) Keep records of what you plant, when, weather and soil conditions, successes and failures. It saves money and time over the long haul.

10) Consider planting honeysuckle, persimmons, apples and other deer foods around plot perimeters. Such plants do well on "edge" openings, and provide deer additional food for not much more hunter effort.

Seed Savvy

You've decided to plant food plots for deer on your hunt property, but what seed should you put in the ground? Wheat? Oats? Rye? Barley? Or one of the dozens of newer, generally better, plot plants designed specifically for wildlife?

Almost anything you sow will help deer and other game. But most wildlife biologists believe the best plants are those high in protein that are very "digestible" to deer and tolerant of the geographic location. This can be confusing, because there are at least 100 different types of plants used for wildlife in the southeastern U.S. alone.

The easiest way to help choose what to plant on your land is to check with other local hunters and learn what works for them. Decide if you want to plant in spring-summer or fall-winter. Next, let the soil analysis lead you to the best seeds. Many plant varieties have very specific needs, like dry or loamy soil; some need lots of rain, and some require more sun than others.

Decide, too, whether you're planting solely for deer, or if you also want plants that aid turkeys, quail, pheasants, even ducks and rabbits.

The Pennington Seed Company of Madison, Georgia publishes a Wild Game Catalog with a wealth of information on plot seed selection. It recommends when certain seeds should be planted according to geographic location, lists what animals the plants are best for, and how much seed is needed per acre, and offers fertilizing tips and evaluations of dozens of seed types.

Plants extra-high in protein are choice for deer food plots. Mossy Oak's BioLogic and the Whitetail Institute's Imperial Whitetail Cover, Imperial No-Plow and Alfa-Rack are all plot plants getting rave reviews from hunters and game managers.

Some biologists recommend hunters use a mix of wildlife seeds for plots. Seed mixes are available from companies like Pennington, or you can mix your own, combining various clovers and alfalfas, for example. A good seed mix helps ensure against complete crop failure due to rain, drought, frost, etc.

Another way to plant a plot is to put, say, BioLogic on one area of the site, with Imperial Cover in another section, and Pennington Deer Mix in yet a third region. Such a seed "mix" should ensure deer on your hunt property get plenty of nutrition, and they'll be there during hunting season, too.

Planting deer food plots takes time, effort, and money. But it's effort well spent for buster bucks. CREDIT FIDUCCIA ENTERPRISES.

Get the Weeds Out

Anyone who has a yard or garden knows how tenacious weeds are and how tiresome it is to keep them at bay. It's the same with deer food plots, and don't believe some magic herbicide is available to do the work for you. It isn't.

"There are very few herbicides registered for use on forages planted for whitetail deer, and most are available only to commercial applicators," explains Dr. W. Carroll Johnson, a plant authority formerly with the University of Georgia. "Depending exclusively on herbicides to control weeds is neither environmentally nor economically wise."

Site preparation is an important part of "weed management." Disking a plot several times over several weeks, then applying the correct and adequate lime and fertilizers, followed by plenty of the very best seed, is the smartest thing a hunter can do to get a good plot crop and keep weeds to a minimum.

Tilling, mowing, and hand roughing can be done to keep weeds at bay as your food plot matures.

"Hand-weeding forage plots may be the most practical and effective means to manage weeds, especially sporadic or patchy weeds in small food plots," Johnson continues. "When used as the final step in an integrated weed management system, 'touching up' with

Not many herbicides are available for deer forage plants. CREDIT FIDUCCIA ENTERPRISES.

hand-weeding may be practical and very effective." >

Hanging Tree Stands Right

WITH JIM JONES

"Where and how you hang a tree stand may determine if the buck of your dreams will work into bow range."

J im Jones of Jacksonville, Florida, worked his way up the giant white oak trunk. He reached the top of the 20-foot, strap-on mini-ladder and trimmed a few dead twigs with a folding saw. Then he looked down at his companion and motioned for him to hand up the lock-on tree stand.

Jim's buddy climbed eight or 10 feet up the ladder and pushed the stand seat up toward his outstretched arms. When Jim grabbed the top of the stand, his hunting companion quickly got back down on the ground and stepped out of harm's way.

He had helped Jim scout the oak ridge, locating trails and scrapes, rubs and tracks from feeding deer. The two checked wind direction, and Jim decided on a large-trunk white oak tree 20 yards from a trail crossing on the ridge side. It was a great location—uphill and downwind from where Jim expected to see deer. His pal thought the spot was a "sure deer" with a bow, and thought Jim had gone bonkers when he attached the stand to the back of the tree.

The friend motioned to Jim to set the stand on the downhill side of the tree, so he'd face the trails below. But ignoring his companion, Jim worked to attach his stand to the uphill side of the oak.

Finally, the friend couldn't keep silent any longer, and whispered in a quiet deer-woods voice—but loud enough that Jim would hear (assuming nearby whitetails wouldn't).

"Where are you hanging that stand? How are you gonna see and shoot deer with your stand facing uphill, on the opposite side of the tree where bucks will approach?"

Jim didn't respond; he just smiled at his friend and calmly went about his business. Then he climbed down and quietly motioned for them to leave the area in silence.

Back at their vehicle, Jim explained his bowhunting plan.

"That white oak has no big limb cover low, under my stand, so I'd stick out like a black bear on a white flag pole if I put that stand facing deer trails downhill," Jim told his friend as they pulled away from the woods toward town and lunch. "By putting the stand facing uphill, 180 degrees away from where deer will show, I'll be able to use that wide oak tree trunk as cover. I'll hunt standing up, watching trails downhill and behind my tree. I'll be able to draw my bow, lean around the trunk and shoot without deer spotting any movement—thanks to that oversize white oak."

And that's just what happened that afternoon, when the pair of hunters went back to their respective bow stands. The friend arrowed a doe right at dusk, while Jim zipped a nice two-and-a-half-year-old eight-pointer. His buck was a few minutes behind three does that walked one of the trails, unaware of Jim behind the oak tree, concealing his stand and body—at least until he loosed his arrow.

Such simple things about where and how to use tree stands can make a significant difference in bowhunting success—especially when pur-

Having limbs and leaves around a tree stand to "break up" a bowhunter outline is important to success.

suing older deer that have survived several seasons, says Jim. Those old whitetails, particularly battle-worn bucks, are well tuned to the ways of hunters. So you're wise to go the extra yard in positioning tree stands and preparing an "advanced" timber-top ambush.

"Veteran archers spend so much time walking and scouting, poring over maps and aerial photos, listening to reports from other hunters, farmers, ranchers, and anyone else who has important whitetail data, that when finally a great spot is located for hunting, all too often bowmen leap too quickly in setting up a tree stand," Jim states. "That can be a costly mistake."

Jim says that once you've located a choice spot to hunt, one of the most important parts of hanging any tree stand is stopping a moment and deliberately thinking about the ambush. Imagine deer meandering through the area you've chosen to watch, then carefully visualize where the best spot is in the treetops for a stand, he advises.

"Once you've located a hot trail, deer crossing, series of scrapes or rubs, the obvious hard work is over," reports Jim. "But you haven't closed the deal until you've pinpointed the best tree to attach your stand. Take your time choosing the exact spot to complete a perfect hunt. First order of business is to check the wind, of course. Be sure to choose a stand site where the prevailing wind is blowing away from the area you expect to see game.

"That usually narrows tree choices considerably, but once you've got the wind 'corridor' located, you can start the process of tree selection, using a simple process of elimination. You don't want a downwind tree too far from the area you expect to see deer, but you don't want it too close, either. Many veteran bowhunters prefer stands 15 to 25 yards from a spot they believe deer will show."

A good-size tree is preferred—something with a diameter as wide as a hunter's shoulders, which makes it easy to attach most tree stand designs and affords good camouflage. If you're fortunate enough to have a choice of several trees that fulfill these conditions, choose a hardwood over a pine. A pine's sap is messy, and the loose, "leafy" bark can make it noisy. If there are several hardwoods to pick from, find one with a straight trunk to make setup easy, and with large, low limbs, vines, and leafy cover to conceal a hunter.

"I like having a big limb or two under my stand base, as well as large, leafy cover around my torso when I'm in the stand," Jim says, "because as all good bowhunters know only too well, deer do look up. Any time you can place a stand in a multi-trunk tree, you have found one of the ultimate sites for bowhunting."

Sometimes positioning a tree stand on the opposite side of a tree where you expect deer is wise. This way the tree trunk affords cover from animals approaching the stand.

Most experienced archers know only too well that much of the time there's no "perfect" tree available. Crooked trees are a real pain, but that can be dealt with by using ladder-type stands. Some sophisticated adjustable-base stands allow for platforms and seats to be made level, even when the stand support is cockeyed because of the tree's uneven shape.

Huge-trunk oaks and ones without low limb cover are a challenge for bowhunting, too. Some trees are so big that getting a lock-on chain or strap around them is almost impossible. Sometimes an additional "add-on" chain or strap can be used, or an alternate lean-on ladder stand can be employed (though more chain/strap may be needed, too).

For cover, set a stand on the opposite side of the tree from where you expect to see deer—using the big trunk for camouflage. Climbing extra high in such trees is also a good idea—with 20 feet about minimum; if possible, it's smart to get up at least as high as the first low, large limbs. This also can aid getting a strap or chain around a big-trunk tree, as the higher you climb, the smaller the trunk becomes.

Add-on camouflage can be an important part of stand concealment for bowhunters working from tough-to-hide-in trees. Sometimes it's possible to cut a few large, leafy limbs and position them around a stand base, or even strap them to a trunk to help "break" a bowman's outline. Almost any type of natural cover can help, but pine or fir boughs are best because they stay green longer, and the natural pungent fragrance of their sap helps mask human scent. Limbs can be tied to stands with cord, elastic straps, electrician's tape, or simply wedged in the slots or straps of your stand base.

One of the easiest ways to add camouflage around an otherwise "open" tree stand is with imitation foliage. There are some commercially made plastic "branches" designed specifically for hunting on the market, and similar ones sold, inexpensively, in craft stores. Most have wire stems that are easily wound around stands and attached to trees. Just a few such fake "limbs," strategically located near a stand base or in a tree trunk to the sides of a bowhunter, "break" his outline so that he becomes invisible to deer. The beauty of imitation foliage is that it's small, lightweight, and will fit easily in a hunter's daypack.

Bowhunters camouflage tree stands with everything from brown burlap cloth to green canvas awnings, camouflage tee shirts to special "Leaf-O-Flage" blind material.

It all works, but it can be difficult to deal with. To do it right, you'll need more material than you thought necessary, and it's got to attach snugly, yet not so tight that it doesn't look natural. The specially made blind material is best, and you can buy it in bulk rolls from mail-order houses, particularly those catering to waterfowl hunters. All-black plastic "cable

Anytime a "multi-trunk" tree can be used for a tree stand, it should be chosen over other hunting locations.

ties" work well to fasten such material to limbs and branches around a stand, or to the stand base itself.

A number of companies produce add-on or after-market camouflage blinds for tree-stand use. One type has a 27-inch high cloth camo blind that attaches to a stand base. In use, it flares up and out from the base, looking much like a tulip, so the blind material doesn't interfere with an archer. It almost completely hides a sitting hunter, but a standing archer has no trouble shooting over it.

Another innovative camouflage aid available consists of a cluster of artificial plastic limbs and leaves, which have a bendable wire fitted through them. The unit has four or six "branches" flaring out from a tapered block; they can be bent to any angle or shape, and the block to which they are fitted easily slides into a bracket that straps to a tree trunk or limb. In use, the strap and bracket are positioned to the side or behind a tree strand, then the block with artificial branches and leaves is snapped into place. You simply bend the wires of the "branches" wherever cover is needed around, to the sides, and under a stand, and you're well camouflaged.

Another simple attachment that can be used to break a bowman's outline is a camouflage umbrella. Most hunters purchase such camo-colored umbrellas as a shield for rain or sun. But large ones, up to 54 inches, strategically positioned in a limbless tree, can simulate foliage and conceal a hunter.

"While a good tree-stand rule of thumb is to always position stands above the first large limb or two of a tree, it is possible to hang a stand so high that foliage reduces visibility and impairs hunting effectiveness," reports Jim. "In such a case, you're better off setting a stand well below tree limbs—and maybe using 'add-on' camouflage to conceal your movements from ever-wary whitetails.

"Also, it's helpful to have a friend help hang a tree stand. Get in the stand and look at the spots you believe you'll get shots at deer. Have your friend help trim out shooting lanes with a pole saw or pruning shears. It's fast and much better than trying to do it on your own."

Jim favors hunting thick, dense cover, which he says harbors most wary whitetails. He prefers hunting the heart of such thickets, or on the edges closest to feed areas, like oak ridges and agricultural fields.

"Midday hunting can be outstanding in thick places where you have a stand positioned correctly," he believes. If the weather is good and cool on a public hunting area, I'd rather hunt from 9 a.m. to 3 p.m. than any other time of day—especially during a full moon." >

Jim Jones owns Jim's Archery Shop in Jacksonville, Florida, and is a widely traveled bowman. He has over 40 years of bow deer hunting experience, having collected more than 200 public-land whitetails. His best deer is an Iowa buck scoring 158 inches, and he has taken eight deer large enough to be included in the prestigious Pope & Young Club.

Play the Angles

"Bowhunting from tree stands is an advanced course in geometry."

The Illinois buck showed about mid-morning 100 yards away on the opposite side of the draw Vicki Cianciarulo was bowhunting. Her tree stand was high, positioned near a hole in a fence that paralleled a deep ravine 20 yards away and well below her feet. She expected deer to walk the trail on her side of the ravine, along the hardwood ridge where her stand was set. A number of scrapes around her tree stand showed bucks were working the ridge near the fence hole; she just didn't expect a buck to walk near the ravine along the opposite ridge.

Vicki softly grunted on her deer call, and though the buck never stopped or looked her way, he started angling down his ridge toward the fence. He was still 70 yards out, but Vicki could see he was a nice eight-pointer—one she'd take if he offered a good shot. At 50 yards, he was still moving along his side of the draw, looking like he was leaving the area. She grunted again, louder this time, and the buck turned to the fence.

Vicki knew the distance to the fence hole from her tree stand was 20 yards; the eight-pointer was beyond that spot. If he reached the fence beyond the hole, she figured he'd be 30 yards away, but very low in the ravine. So low, in fact, that when the deer stopped broadside at the fence and Vicki came to full draw, she hesitated for a second about where to hold her bow sight pin. She automatically put the 30-yard pin behind the buck's shoulder, but seeing the steep angle down to him, she raised the pin and aimed just under his spine.

Vicki touched the released, the bow recoiled, and she watched the white vanes from her carbon arrow disappear high and down into the buck's chest. In a flash, the eight-pointer was over the fence, and for a second Vicki thought she'd made a bad hit, striking much too high. The deer ran up the hill toward Vicki's stand, around it, and turned to head back into the ravine. But he folded, dead before hitting the ground, just 10 yards from her tree, going only 40 yards from the fence before succumbing.

"The 'high' hit I made actually had been perfect," she recalls. "The buck was so far below my stand in the ditch, that the steep angle needed to send my broadhead through the center of his chest required that it strike

Vicki Cianciarulo took this large Colorado whitetail by knowing how to aim arrows in rolling terrain. CREDIT ARCHER'S CHOICE MEDIA, INC.

very high in the kill zone, just under the spine. If I'd hit the buck where I usually aim, low center, behind the shoulder, it's possible the broadhead would have traveled way too low in the chest, and his rack would have been just a memory rather than a trophy on display in my office."

Learning "all the angles" for arrows to properly strike deer from tree stands comes only from experience—always the best outdoor teacher. But bowhunters can learn a lot by practicing on 3-D targets at home or at a local archery range, says Vicki, veteran whitetail hunter and outdoor television personality.

"Another fast way to help learn arrow angles on big game is by using a small, toy-size, full-dimensional deer," she says, "though any four-legged toy animal will do—horse, pig, dog, bear, etc. A budding tree-stand bowhunter can teach himself a lot about where arrows must be aimed according to where and how a little fake deer stands in relation to an imaginary tree-stand hunter.

"Place the toy deer [horse, pig, etc.] broadside, eye-level on a table. Picture where an arrow should strike the toy, behind the shoulder, for a quick kill. Turn the toy 30 degrees away. Where would you aim now? Now turn it 45 degrees, now 60 degrees. Now slowly stand up, increasing the height above the toy on the table. Notice how the spot of arrow impact changes according to the angle the animal is turned, and your height above it? Now take a step closer to the table. Move back two steps. Start to get the picture[s]?"

Vicki says it may sound obvious, but an arrow should always be driven through the center chest of a deer. This salient point is vital every time a bowman draws on a buck—because the aim angle to the center chest target varies dramatically according to the distance of the deer, and how it is positioned. For example, she says, a buck standing broadside at 30 yards is no problem for most bowmen in tree stands. It's the perfect shot, easy down angle, and simple to place a broadhead where it needs to be.

But the same broadside buck closer to a stand, say, just five yards from the tree, poses an entirely different target angle, with unique aiming problems. The angle down to the five-yard deer is much more acute, Vicki states, so a bowhunter must aim higher in the "kill zone" to effectively drive an arrow through the deer's center chest. The angle and aim point change even more dramatically if the buck is standing other than broadside.

"A deer at very close range, almost under a stand, seems like a chip shot for many bowhunters, though usually only to those who have not had to make this shot—which I think is one of the most difficult in all bowhunting," Vicki explains. "The bow is best drawn from a level position, then a hunter bends at the waist and leans over to aim [it's suicidal without a safety belt]. If the deer is facing away, showing only its back, the aim point is between the shoulder blades, perhaps just a bit back, which angles the broadhead forward and through the center chest of the animal.

"A buck in the same below-stand position, but facing the hunter, presents an entirely different angle to get an arrow through the center chest. His head must be low, in a feeding position, for this shot to effective. If the deer's head is up, and the animal is alert, a hunter should wait for it to pass beneath his stand, then make the going-away-and-down shot. But if the facing deer's head is down, and close, the angle for arrow entry is between the shoulders, and just a bit forward. You want the broadhead to exit the deer's underside chest, not out through the paunch, which can make trailing very difficult."

Some years ago, Vicki was hunting a great Midwest spot with lots of deer and some good bucks. She set a stand over some rubs and a trail crossing, and that afternoon had deer all around her. Does, yearlings and small bucks wandered under her feet, and the pressure not to be picked off by their eyes and ears was intense, especially when a dandy 10-pointer stepped out at 45 yards. He was following a spike, walking in his every step, and they were coming directly to Vicki, the 130-class Pope & Young 10-pointer about 20 yards behind the spike.

Understanding where a deer's vital areas are located helps to properly envision where an arrow should be placed.

The small buck stopped under her stand, the big boy at 20 yards, but facing her, head up. Vicki was ready to draw. All the buck had to do was turn, giving her the right angle. She could have taken the straight-on shot, directly into the chest, but an exit wound from such a hit is bad news; almost no blood trail is a likely result. She waited for the 10-pointer to turn or come under her stand, like the spike had done. But something spooked him and he was gone in a flash, along with the rest of the deer around her stand.

"I berated myself for not taking the straight-on shot, since the buck was so close, missing his heart would have been difficult," she recalls. "But I made the right choice in not shooting. An arrow off by only an inch with that poor target angle, and the broadhead does not exit well. And following a mortally wounded deer without a blood trail is extremely difficult, especially in thick woods, which it was.

Bowmen must be aware of a deer's large shoulder bone on this shot, and also understand the downward angle, to send a broadhead through the center of the chest.

"A bowman must envision an arrow as it passes into and through a deer in order to pick the ideal broadhead-impact spot. One way to imagine this is to view a picture of a buck from above, and mark the four corners of the compass around the deer—east, west, north and south. If the buck is facing north, a straight-line arrow from east or west is ideal. Any arrow angle from just slight north or south from due east or west also is satisfactory, though it quickly becomes evident that the entrance point for an arrow must be adjusted slightly in order for the shaft to pass through the center chest of the buck."

Vicki explains that an arrow hitting the deer from due south (its rump) is a poor shot, naturally, because it must pass through a ham or paunch before reaching the forward chest and vitals. But if the deer is turned at a slight angle, even 30 degrees off due north, an arrow striking the deer almost anywhere along its side,

The so-called "quartering-away" shot angle is perfect for deer from tree stands.

except way forward, will pass through the center chest. This is why, she states, the so-called "quartering-away" shot angle is perfect for deer from tree stands. A buck looking away at about a 45- to 60-degree angle is in grave jeopardy of a skilled archer. Conversely, a buck quartering toward a bowhunter offers a poor shot, because the animal's large shoulder bones prevent broadhead penetration into the center chest. In such a situation, an archer should wait for an animal to turn and offer a better arrow angle to the kill zone, Vicki describes.

"All of these broadside, quartering-away, quartering-to, etc., aim-point angles are complicated even more according to the height of a hunter's tree stand and the distance the animal is from a hunter," Vicki says. "Tree-stand height can dramatically alter aim-point angle. I know plenty of archers who regularly place stands 25, even 30 feet up, sometimes higher. I've hunted from such heights, and while sometimes it's necessary, shooting down from 30 feet greatly increases arrow angle to a target. By climbing that high, you're effectively reducing the target size of an animal's vital area. The so-called 'pie-plate' size target of a broadside deer at 20 yards from a 15-foot high tree stand quickly becomes half that size when you double the stand height."

Deer don't fly, laughs Vicki, but sometimes in hilly terrain a whitetail can show above a tree stand hunter.

"I've had this happen out West, and friends who hunt West Virginia and parts of the Northeast say this isn't unusual," Vicki says seriously. "You can hang a stand on a hillside, for example, hunting a creek draw below your feet, only to have a buck walk above you on the ridge top. This, of course, creates an unusual target angle for a bowhunter. In the extreme, the arrow-impact spot may actually be below the centerline of a buck. The arrow may enter in the soft area below the shoulder, traveling up through the center chest . . . and out above the shoulder or near the spine on the opposite side.

"Weird angle, strange situation, but in the mountains, be ready for it. I've taken a couple of nice Western bucks shooting just this way from mountain tree stands."

While tree-stand angles for bowmen can be tricky almost any time, Vicki says to pay special attention to moving or spooky deer. During the rut, it's common for does to be scooting around a stand hunter, with a buck or two in hot pursuit. It's exciting and great fun when this happens, but Vicki says a hunter's mental "arrow-angle calculator" had best be working overtime. Spot the buck you want out there broadside at 35 yards, then suddenly he chases a young buck or a doe right under your stand, and the behind-the-shoulder shot you'd planned on suddenly becomes a straight-down, angling-away shot.

"Practice those angles on a 3-D range," advises Vicki. "One day, you'll be glad you did." >

Vicki Cianciarulo, producer of Archer's Choice *television show and videos, travels extensively bowhunting with her husband, Ralph. She's an accomplished archer who has taken numerous big-game animals, including three record-book black bears, African kudu and eland, as well as more than 30 whitetail deer. She lives in Illinois, where she tagged her biggest buck to date, a massive 11-pointer with over 156-inches of rack.*

PART THREE

FINDING WHITETAILS

Hunting Wild Fruit

WITH MIKE MOONEY

"When these wild succulent fruits are ripe and falling, the deer dinner bell is definitely ringing. Hunters should heed that sound, too."

Years ago on a special three-day, permit-only public bowhunt, Jacksonville, Florida bowhunter Mike Mooney and a friend were wearing out their boot soles scouting for deer sign. The place was big and fertile, and they quickly found plenty of spots to hang stands. Mike decided to hunt a field corner where several trails led up from a steep draw. Shortly after daybreak the first morning of the hunt, he zipped a fat doe there, which immediately spun around and raced back into the bottom from which she came.

Mike heard her fall and marked the spot. Limit on that hunt was three deer, so he waited on stand for a

Be sure to "back trail" doe tracks leading to open, obvious fruit trees in fields or around old farms. Often, as you get closer to heavier cover, you'll discover buck sign.

couple more hours, passing two more does before climbing down to track and recover his deer.

As so often happens when trailing a shot animal, that doe led Mike to an area honeycombed with fresh deer trails and sign. He quickly found several new spots to relocate his stand while trailing the doe, when he suddenly broke out of a hillside thicket onto a flat, open area that was unusual for the region. It was kind of a hardwood "bench" surrounded by thickets and brambles, and as Mike looked about, he stepped on something squishy. His feet suddenly slid out from under him, and he promptly landed on his butt, holding out his hands to break his fall. His fingers buried into a mushy blanket of over-ripe crab apples that literally covered the ground.

Never before, nor since, had Mike seen crab apples like that. There were three squat trees so heavy with fruit, some of the limbs had cracked from weight. Thousands of apples blanketed the ground. There was so much pungent fruit rotting at Mike's feet, he thought it impossible deer could be eating it. But that theory quickly evaporated when he started looking carefully between the apples, and noted that the soil was also covered with whitetail droppings.

If there was ever a woods sign that screamed "put your tree stand here," that was it. So that afternoon Mike sat high in a nearby oak 25 yards from the mini-orchard, and had plenty of time to survey the spot. He came to believe it was an old homestead, and either the planted apple trees had gone wild, or they were wild trees the former inhabitants had nurtured. There were no old buildings nearby, nor dilapidated foundations. But the place was too perfect a level spot, the trees too ripe with fruit, for man not to have had a hand in the growing of those abundant apples.

An hour or so after Mike settled in the stand, the first deer showed, a doe and two yearlings. They fed for 30 minutes, finally bedding down under his feet beside the oak tree. Two more solo does showed up next, followed by two bucks—a large-body spike and bigger four-pointer. It being a limited, three-day public hunt, the bucks were tempting targets. But Mike decided to wait, as he had two more full days of bowhunting.

It was one of the best woods decisions he ever made.

An hour before dark, a heavy, mature six-pointer showed, and Mike put a three-blade broadhead high through both the buck's lungs, watching him fall less than 50 yards from the orchard. At dusk, a slightly smaller eight-point buck with a nice wide rack appeared, and Mike dumped him, too.

Mike's pal helped him haul out the deer, and he aided his buddy in carting out a doe he'd shot from a distant stand.

Mike had filled his limit on the area, so his pal hunted the apple orchard stand the next morning. He shot a doe and the four-pointer Mike had seen the previous afternoon.

"Why didn't you hold out for another buck," Mike asked his pal as they dragged out the doe.

"You took two bucks yesterday, and I figured I'd better get my deer and we'd head home," countered Mike's friend. "Heck, we've already contaminated the area a lot with human activity."

"Uh huh, well look," Mike whispered, pointing to the apple orchard as they skirted 75 yards from it downwind dragging out the doe.

There, under the oak where Mike's stand was still hanging, was another eight-pointer, much bigger and with a wider rack than the one he'd dropped the previous day.

Sometimes the moon and stars align just right for bowhunters, and that trip some years ago was just such an outing for Mike. But over the years, there have been a lot of successful whitetail trips like that because Mike found wild fruit that deer were feasting on.

This isn't to say that every tree loaded with crab apples, persimmons, wild plums or grapes is an automatic spot to arrow deer, according to Mike. Nothing is that certain. In fact, he has found some fruit in prime deer areas that just didn't attract game. He doesn't know why this is so. Perhaps a pear tree loaded with fruit, with no deer feeding on it, simply hasn't been discovered by animals yet. Or perhaps some fruit trees are just not preferred by deer. Whatever the reason, don't be lured to fruit and assume deer are a pushover there.

Still, Mike believes the odds are good that when a bowman locates abundant wild fruit, he has discovered a hot spot to hang a stand and harvest deer.

Wild fruits are among the most important foods for deer during early bow season, explains Mike, because it's often available to game long before acorns are ripe or corn fields mature. Further, by the time most firearms seasons roll around, fruit has long since fallen and been consumed by whitetails. Thus, areas that draw deer and hold them for their fruity foods are pretty much the sole domains of bowhunters.

Locating wild fruits can be as challenging as finding any other preferred natural deer food, like acorns or choice browse. There's little substitute for wearing out your boot soles in scouting for fruit, but don't do all your looking at the ground. Often, the very best fruit trees have little or

When you locate a spot having concentrated tracks, turn your eyes up and look for trees bearing fruit.

no fruit near your feet. A persimmon tree or grapevine hammered by feeding deer rarely has fruit laying under it—which is why Mike was so surprised at the deer productivity of the apple orchard described at the beginning of this chapter. Wild fruit usually doesn't last long once it hits terra firma. If deer don't eat it, raccoons, foxes, opossums and insects do.

"That's why it's important to keep your eyes open to 'feed' sign on the ground," explains Mike. "Deer droppings and tracks are obvious, but sometimes the soil will be stomped heavily, and leaves and sticks will be flipped around unusually from animals 'nosing' under it like they do for acorns. When you locate a spot having concentrated tracks, droppings and 'flipped' leaves, turn your eyes up and look for trees bearing fruit. Binoculars help, and if the site is slightly inclined, be sure to look uphill, since apples, pears, plums and grapes roll.

"If you find a tree bearing fruit, with deer sign on the ground but no fruit down for deer to eat, take time to shake the tree and its limbs. Knock as much fruit as possible to the ground to attract deer. I've actually climbed trees to cut out fruit, careful not to use my hands, but employing a hand saw or machete to keep from contaminating the fruit with human scent. Grapes on tall, winding vines can be tough to reach. I have a friend who uses a pole saw for trimming tall fruit trees and clipping off ripe grapes on vines winding through timber."

Mike says some of the best-bearing fruit trees are found around homesteads, near woods openings and field edges. Such trees yield a lot of fruit because sunlight can reach them well, which helps plants to flower—and for each flower there is fruit. Many such fruit trees also benefit from fertilizers, either from old homesteads, or because they're growing beside active farm fields.

"Some of the most fruit-heavy apple and persimmon trees you'll find are in fence rows between fields, and around field edges," Mike continues. "I've even found giant fruit

Binoculars help you spot fruit high in trees to learn its availability. Be sure to mark tree locations on a map for later reference.

trees growing beside old dirt roads in prime deer country. Many such spots in the comparative open have lots of deer tracks and droppings under them. Because deer must walk across open fields, they're usually visited at night. Yet you still can hunt such 'open' fruit spots. Just 'back track' trails to where deer are leaving a thicket, point of hardwoods, or pine plantation, and set a stand there.

"I once found a fruit-heavy muscadine grape vine loaded with deer sign growing beside a rural South Carolina school house. Closest woods were behind the building, some 200 yards away. I walked the woods edge, located two deer trails emerging from the timber and heading to the grapes. I hung a stand between the two trails, 50 yards back in the woods, and arrowed a fat doe the first afternoon. That deer showed up early, simply milling around in the timber, apparently waiting for sundown before heading across the open to the school house for a grape dinner."

Fruit trees in open areas are notorious for attracting does, and some bowhunters shun them for that reason. But such spots draw bucks, too, because as the rut approaches, ladies attract gentlemen. Be sure to "back trail" doe tracks leading to open, obvious fruit trees in fields or around old farms. Often, as you get closer to heavier cover, you'll discover buck sign. It may be several hundred yards from where fruit trees are growing, but bucks, does and yearlings are holding in the area because of the food.

Don't overlook fruit trees in suburban areas, advises Mike, because plenty of buster bucks come to backyard apple, plum and peach trees. And in the West, juicy apples are high on the menu of mule deer and whitetails.

One of the easiest and quickest ways to locate fruit trees for hunting is to look for them in spring, when the trees flower. This often coincides with spring gobbler season, so if you're chasing toms, keep a sharp eye out for wild fruit trees in bloom. Apple, pear and plum trees tend to be especially loaded with blooms, and when trees bud out in all that colorful glory, you can bank on them bearing fruit—remember, each little flower is an apple or pear, plum or peach.

"Make sure you have a quality topographical map with you when locating fruit trees in spring," Mike says. "After trees lose their blossoms and return to their green-leaf state, they blend right in with habitat and can be a challenge to find unless you've recorded their location on a map, or used a portable GPS navigation unit to pinpoint them. Sometimes a number of trees will be in a wide area, so don't be completely satisfied and set your stand if you discover just one tree dropping fruit. Often, another tree or two just 50 or 100 yards away will have even more deer sign.

"Deer often have decided preferences for one grape vine or a particular apple tree—just like they do for acorns from a special oak tree. Only reason I can think this occurs is because fruit from a preferred tree simply tastes better to game. You can 'sweeten' such trees and grapevines easily by adding fertilizer to plants. A bag of 10-10-10 fertilizer, Scotts 'Tree Tablets' or 'Native Plant' fertilizer will not only strengthen chosen fruit trees, but they'll bear more fruit, and game will go nuts over them."

Mike says judicious pruning of wild fruit trees can help yield more and better quality fruit that deer most desire. A pole cutter, hand saw and pruning shears can be used to quickly cut away dead limbs and unwanted trunk sprouts. Trim off long "leggy" limbs and remove brush from around tree trunks so the soil nutrients aren't sapped by weeds and other low cover. If you're really industrious, cut back taller trees around the area to allow more sunlight to reach a fruit tree, fostering more blossoms and yield.

A few handfuls of fertilizer around the "drip line," and a tree should be well on its way to producing plenty of fruit, and drawing deer from near and far, Mike contends. This kind of woods work is minimal, and really pays off during years when woods mast is scarce, since "nurtured" fruit trees tend to bear more and better fruit when other wild trees have little production.

In certain regions of America, there are localized "fruits" attractive to deer, says Mike. For example, in Florida, palmettos at times bear large berries that, when ripe and dark black, are an important draw for deer. Gallberries in much of the South are important, too. Mike has never hunted around wild cherries, but has been told by bowhunting pals they can attract whitetails.

"One of the most unique 'fruits' I ever heard about hunting around was in the low-country region of South Carolina, near the town of Estill," details Mike. "A friend found the place by accident one September afternoon while scouting for deer. He walked into a natural woods clearing, and growing there were wild watermelons. Most had been cracked open, and deer tracks all around them proved conclusively that whitetails had kicked open the melons and were feasting on the sweet meat."

Mike's pal hung a tree stand near the wild melon patch, and shot a six-point buck that first afternoon.

"I've never hunted near watermelons, and had no idea they could be so productive for deer," Mike says. "My buddy figures someone had eaten a watermelon there in the woods and the discarded seeds grew into a pretty fair patch. He knew the spot had potential for deer hunting, so he nurtured the place by planting more seeds and periodically fertilizing and even weeding the patch. The place now covers about an acre, and the melons are huge thanks to fertilizing. My friend gets a South Carolina deer there just about every season, including a 16-inch spread nine-pointer last year.

"Since then he's planted, fertilized and grown two more small melon patches in other regions he hunts. All of 'em—and I mean all of 'em—produce deer for my pal."

Where to Get Plants & Seeds

Hunters can transplant wild persimmon, apple, pear, and even oak trees to choice hunting locations. It's best done when plants are dormant, without leaves, from late autumn to early spring. Young plants or "babies" are available from some types of wild plants, like persimmons, as they grow up from the parent tree root system. Be sure to get a young plant's entire "root ball," and it's wise to plant several young trees or bushes in a choice hunting location to ensure success, since not all plants survive.

Some plants, like honeysuckle, apple, and pear trees, are available from nurseries, and they're not particularly expensive.

The Wildlife Group in Tuskegee, Alabama, sells plants suitable for enhancing whitetail habitat via mail order, such as Japanese honeysuckle, persimmons, crab apples, oaks, olives, pears, chestnuts, and others. The company also offers a brochure guide to wild plantings.

The Whitetail Institute, Pennington Seed Company, and Frigid Forage are a few of the companies that sell wildlife food seeds, and offer expertise on planting various seeds for whitetails in different regions. Check state agencies as well, as many sell wildlife seeds and trees, too.

There are many companies selling wildlife food seeds. Some state agencies sell these types of seeds, too. CREDIT FIDUCCIA ENTERPRISES.

Tools of the Trade

You may feel more like a farmer than a bowhunter, but sportsmen who want to enhance fruit trees on whitetail property should have the following:

1. A spade for digging up mature plants and for placing them and shrubs in new locations.
2. A hand trowel for transplanting and digging holes for tree fertilizing.
3. A spreader of some type for broadcasting seeds and/or fertilizer. Some small hand-crank spreaders fasten around the shoulders or neck and work nicely. Standard walk-behind lawn spreaders also can be used.
4. Binoculars to help you locate important whitetail wild fruits like apples and pears in spring, when they're blooming, and to help you spot mature fruit (apples, persimmons, etc.) in treetops during autumn.
5. A detailed topo map of hunt property—important for marking the locations of deer food sources. Make copious notes so sites can be easily located again for hunting and for an ongoing program of fertilizing, pruning and nurturing.
6. A portable GPS navigation unit, especially useful for pinpointing wild fruit-bearing plants in remote areas.
7. Red flagging material for "marking" and keeping track of plants that have been fertilized. This is particularly helpful if many plants in your hunt area have been enhanced over a wide area. >

Mike Mooney, of Jacksonville, Florida, has over 30 years bowhunting experience and 100 big-game animals to his archery credit, including several oversize Pope & Young whitetail bucks. For many years he owned and operated an archery pro shop, and is on the pro staff of PSE Archery.

Nutty Bucks

"When acorns fall, heavy-horned whitetails are vulnerable."

I t was opening weekend of the bow deer season in west-central Alabama, and Jake Markris was in a favorite white oak tree stand near a slough and whitetail bedding area. He knew the place well, and believed it to be a choice big-buck hangout. At 9:30 a.m. he'd already seen a number of does and yearlings, small bucks, wild hogs and turkeys, but no good bucks.

"A timber company started their tree cutting at 9 a.m. about 400 yards away," Jake remembers. "So I was just about ready to climb down from my stand, not believing a buck would come to feed on my white oak with all that human commotion. That's when I spotted movement 200 yards away on an old logging road. I put my binoculars on him and saw he was a shooter buck. He was moving pretty quickly, at least for a buck, and he came right to my tree. There was no doubt that buck had his heart set on feasting on white oak acorns pouring out of my tree."

At 20 yards the buck turned broadside, Jake drew his bow, anchored, and sent a broadhead through both its lungs. The wide, high-rack eight-pointer was still in velvet—a rare trophy for Alabama bowmen—and he was down for good within seconds. The six-and-a-half-year-old, 160-pound buck had 5¾-inch bases, an 18-inch spread, and would score just under the Pope & Young book minimum—a heck of a deer for Alabama.

One year later, to the exact day, Jake again was in the same white oak tree stand. Again the tree was dropping large, succulent, green acorns, and that afternoon he shot a heavy nine-pointer at 18 yards as the buck and several does fed on ripe nuts.

Jake's white oak tree is a special spot, attracting bucks and dozens of whitetails from miles around. But it's far from a unique place. In truth, when oak trees are raining acorns, few foods are more attractive to whitetails—especially bucks. Acorns are one of the most protein-rich foods deer can get, which puts the nuts high on a whitetail-preferred menu.

"When white oak acorns are falling, there's nothing deer want more," says Jake, smiling as he remembers his tree-stand hot spot and the deer he has taken there over the years. "I've got so many hot tree stands that produce deer because of acorns that I can hardly remember all of them."

Few wildlife foods attract and concentrate whitetail deer like preferred

Big, round-lobed leaves and oversize acorns are telltale signs of white oaks.

acorns, says Jake. He emphasizes preferred, because not all oak tree mast is equal. The best, by far, are acorns from white oaks and red oaks. Deer big and small rush to them, and bucks are rarely left behind. When such trees aren't available, other oaks fill the bill, and their acorns are sought by deer, too.

"White oaks and red oaks are indigenous throughout the Eastern United States, and everywhere they're found, they are an important source of deer food," states Jake. "I believe when such oak mast is available, deer travel long distances to feed on it, and they will snub otherwise prime foods in favor of white and red oak fruit.

"Many times I've witnessed deer parade across a forest floor covered with acorns from water oaks, turkey oaks and other trees to gorge on a comparatively few white oak acorns. I've seen deer wade through a field of ripe soybeans, cross lush green grass fields, and step out of standing corn to get to bright green white or red oak nuts.

"I am so convinced that white and red oak acorns are such a preferred deer food that whenever I'm scouting for places to hunt, I'm consciously looking for stands of these easily identified trees. A few times I've located a white or red oak dropping nuts that had little deer sign around it. But I believe this is simply because animals hadn't yet discovered the acorns, or there were so many white or red oaks dropping at the same time that deer were not concentrated there. Sometimes repeatedly checking a 'hot' tree is worthwhile, because when deer learn about the nuts, you can bank on them feeding there."

Jake doesn't know for sure why deer have such a thing for white and red oaks, but their acorns are large and presumably extra tasty to deer. Indians reportedly made a bread from white oak acorn meat, which hints at how delectable the fruit must be to whitetails. Another theory is these acorns are extra high in protein and nutrition, so deer selectively feed on them.

Whatever the reasons for whitetail acorn preference, every Eastern deer hunter should take special note of white oaks and red oaks, and learn how to identify them in the field. The *Audubon Society Field Guide to North American Trees (Eastern Region)* is a good reference—very helpful in identifying these oaks as well as other trees that provide deer with important food.

White oaks, common from northern Florida to southern Maine, and from southeast Minnesota to east Texas, are among the easiest of all trees to recognize. Mature trees have a kind of ashen, white cast to their bark, something easily identified once you've seen white oaks on a ridge with pines, hickories and other trees nearby. White oaks also have a very distinctive leaf, with large, rounded lobes.

Red oaks are a bit trickier to identify. There are "northern" and "southern" varieties, and they pretty much cover the East, from Ontario and Maine to Oklahoma, Texas, and Florida. Their leaves have sharper points than white oaks, but they're large, and the bark is dark with deep furrows and ridges. Red oak acorns are huge, too, sometimes well over an inch in length, much like white oak nuts.

Other oaks, like the chestnut oak, are also important to deer, says Jake. Chestnut oaks are huge, with somewhat spear-point shaped, serrated-edge leaves. Their acorns are like white oaks on steroids—some are twice the size of a white oak nut—and whitetails go absolutely, well, nuts for 'em.

"If I find a grove of dropping chestnut oaks—or, as some people call them, chestnut hickory oaks—I can almost guarantee that every deer within a mile is coming to that spot to feed on acorns," states Jake. "It's really incredible what a deer draw they are."

Bur oaks also offer excellent deer mast, and are found throughout the middle third of the nation.

Red, white, chestnut, and bur oaks are large, growing to nearly 100 feet tall, and that oversize is one good way to find them. Also, they often grow on well-drained ridges and the sides of ridges—a notable location, since this is a prime rut region. In some marginal habitats, bur, white and red oaks can be scraggly and not overly productive for acorns. But if they

While not quite as large as a golf ball, chestnut oak acorns are huge, and relished by deer.

Massive chestnut oak acorns dwarf nuts from white oak and overcup oaks. All are deer favorites.

yield nuts, deer will use them.

Many times in many places, Jake has fertilized white and red oaks that unquestionably have produced more acorns that deer seemed to prefer over acorns from other trees he didn't "sweeten." A wide and healthy broadcasting with 6-6-6, 10-10-10, or 13-13-13 fertilizer under a tree's limbs and branches is all it takes. Be aware, however, that this is best done in very early spring, and it often takes a year or two for fertilization to have an appreciable result.

"Fertilizing trees seems to make them yield more acorns and, more importantly, they often have acorns when other oaks have none—which really concentrates deer," reports Jake. "The eight- and nine-point bucks I shot from a white oak tree in succeeding opening day hunts in Alabama were shot on a white oak that I've been fertilizing for six years, and I'm convinced it's made that tree more appealing to whitetails."

Two other oak varieties that can be important deer food sources, especially early in the season, are the water oak and overcup oak, which are especially abundant throughout the Southeast. Experts say water oaks and overcups don't produce the most preferred acorns for deer. But they are consistent producers, usually offering lots of acorns early in the year and during seasons when other oak mast may fail to develop.

Water and overcup oaks thrive in wet, thick areas deer prefer to inhabit. Often, deer "hit" water oaks and/or overcups early in the season, then "pull" off them as white, red, bur, or chestnut oaks begin dropping acorns. Frequently, after they and other animals have consumed all the white, red, bur, and chestnut acorns, whitetails will return to water oaks and overcups. The point here is to stay current with deer sign in your oak hunting areas, and move stands accordingly. Also, just because deer move off water oaks during mid-season, don't be surprised if they return later in the year, when other mast becomes scarce.

One problem with water oaks, however, is that often a "bottom" or creek drainage with such trees has hundreds of oaks "raining" acorns at the same time. Thus, deer can be scattered throughout the low area, which makes it a difficult bowhunting proposition. Some savvy hunters like Jake, however, "sweeten" select water oaks with fertilizer. By spreading fertilizer around a specific tree or two, such trees produce acorns that deer favor, and whitetails are likely to be more concentrated for bowhunting.

There's no special, fast method of locating "hot" oaks. You've simply got to get in the woods and scout, according to Jake. He does a lot of pre-season walking in late summer and just before hunting season, and he's always looking for big oaks. If you find some, be sure to mark their locations on a topographic map, or at least make a notation in a note pad about where you discovered them. If you have a hand-held GPS unit, lock their locations in. Don't leave their positions to memory, since you may have discovered a whitetail gold mine.

This bowhunter has set up a stand in a mature white oak tree, hoping to catch a buck coming in to feed on late-season acorns.

Jake recommends checking trees several times during hunting season. If they're mature and tall, it may help to scan towering branches with binoculars in early fall to learn if the acorn crop is good that year. If you spot acorns in abundance, you're in business, and you might even set a stand before deer traffic becomes heavy. Check the place regularly, every few days, to see if acorns are falling and deer have found them.

"Often acorns are devoured almost as soon as they hit the ground, so don't expect to see plenty of nuts scattered about when scouting a spot," advises Jake. "Look for other 'sign,' like lots of acorn caps [which deer don't eat], droppings, tracks and buck sign. If there's a lot of such sign, it's likely acorns are falling and you'll only rarely find one on the ground because deer are hammering them so fast, the nuts don't stack up like they may in your backyard or a city park. Lots of droppings, fresh tracks and trails, and abundant acorn caps are a sure giveaway for deer ravaging an area for nuts."

How to hunt acorn-bearing oaks depends on the terrain, predominant wind direction, where deer bedding areas are located, and how you walk to and from tree stands. Try to stay well away from an area once you've learned deer are feeding there, says Jake. Setting up downwind or, better, down-and-across-wind, no closer than 20 yards from choice oaks dropping acorns, is a pretty good rule of thumb. And 50 to 100 yards is not too far—depending on the terrain, cover and wind direction.

"Sometimes you may have to hunt oaks where trees are completely out of sight, and you're just overlooking prominent trails leading to acorns from deer bedding areas," says the Alabama hunter. "These days, a lot is made about hunting farm crops and 'green' fields specially planted for deer. While such places are wonderful for whitetails, and plenty of deer are collected in them, when acorns are falling, wise is the hunter who heads to an oak woods—biding his time until a buck shows. And he will." >

Jake Markris, a native of Alabama, travels extensively hunting, and has been on the pro staff of Quaker Boy Game calls for over 15 years. He arrowed his first whitetail at age 17 and has take more than 50 deer with bow and arrows, including a pair of Pope & Young bucks—one from Texas, another from Mississippi.

Deer are creatures of the edge, states veteran and expert bowhunter Harold Knight.

On topo maps, look for four to eight "relief lines" very close together, indicating steep terrain. Next, study the lines, and look for any place where they suddenly widen. This indicates the ridge diminishes in steepness, forming a "pass" or "saddle" that deer may use.

Will Primos arrowed this good buck by grunt calling to it.

In farm country, Terry Head uses binoculars to check doe spots, like woodlot corners tucked back in secluded corn, wheat, soybean and alfalfa fields. When bucks begin seeking does, you've found the hot spots.

The most important part of tree stand selection is wind direction, so as not to spook deer.

Heavy bucks, like this North Dakota brute arrowed by noted bowhunter Vicki Cianciarulo, require bowmen know the correct angles for proper arrow placement. CREDIT ARCHER'S CHOICE MEDIA.

Like his son Chris, Dick Kirby, of western New York, agrees that the best early-season game plan is one that is flexible.

Matt Morrett is a dedicated bow deer hunter with over twenty years experience and more than fifty whitetails to his credit.

Mississippi native Darrell Daigre has taken eight Pope & Young size bucks. He advises during the rut, find a good stand, get there early, and stay there late. CREDIT DARRELL DAIGRE.

Big bucks are common in agricultural areas, and you can produce the same type whitetails by managing your hunting sites with well-managed food plots. CREDIT FIDUCCIA ENTERPRISES.

Take time to locate oaks with abundant acorns poised to drop, as they are likely to draw whitetails.

Hunt the Edges

"Deer are 'edge' oriented. Learn to identify 'edges,' where to find them, how to hunt them, and you'll up your odds for bagging a buck."

Deer are "creatures of the edge." If the average bowhunter kept this one thought in mind while tapping his favorite woodlot or wildlife management area, his success rate on whitetails no doubt would greatly improve.

That insightful hunting tip comes from legendary Tennessee hunter Harold Knight, part of the Knight and Hale Game Call team.

Deer in farm country, mountains, river bottomlands, rolling hills, deserts and swamps all relate to edges, Harold contends. Some edges are very subtle in character and not even obvious to trained hunting eyes. But following edges and relating to them in their daily travel schedule is a normal routine for whitetails everywhere.

This isn't to say that deer only follow edges and never vary from their path, because they do, particularly when spooked or alarmed. But unmolested deer habitually wander along edges.

"Probably the most obvious edge for sportsmen to find and hunt are field perimeters," states Harold. "Check almost any corn, soybean, or other agricultural crop field in deer country, and it becomes quickly obvious that whitetails 'walk the edge.' This is one reason so many deer are shot by hunters around fields.

"Some skeptics state deer hold to edges of such fields because there are choice food crops available to hungry whitetails. But even the edges of fields not having deer forage are attractive to them. Tobacco fields, cotton fields, even barren, freshly plowed fields usually have plenty of whitetail traffic around their edges."

There are a number of reasons why edges attract whitetails, according to Harold. For one, choice browse frequently is found in such places. Honeysuckle, persimmon trees, and plenty of other prime deer foods flourish in the sunlight of field edges. Also, some edges offer deer thick cover to avoid detection from predators.

In addition, certain types of edges—like grown-up fence lines between fields—are natural travel routes for deer as they move from bedding to

Edges are outstanding places to locate heavily traveled deer trails.

feeding areas. Edges also form "lines" that act much like trails for whitetails to follow. An example of such a line is where a stand of mature trees abuts a dog fennel field. Invariably, deer follow such lines because travel is easy, and browse along the tree-field edges is lush and to their liking.

Edges occur in many forms; recognizing them, and knowing how to properly hunt them, takes skill honed by years of experience.

Savvy sportsmen like Harold have learned that a "terrain change"—in other words, an edge—of a hardwood ridge rolling off into a creek bottom is a prime place for deer hunting. The bottom is usually cool with lush green grass and browse, while the ridge side is normally covered with mature hardwoods such as white and red oaks. The bottom typically acts as a secure bedding area, while the ridge is a choice feeding site when acorns are dropping from oaks during autumn. Bowmen who place stands along such edges encounter deer. Ridge-side edges are often among the most consistent places for bucks to make scrape lines to attract does. It's logical to believe bucks scrape in such places because ridgelines are regularly traveled by does, so are therefore prime locations to leave rut calling cards.

"Often more than one edge can be found in any deer hunting area," Harold explains. "In my ridge-creek bottom example, another edge could be found along the creek itself as it winds through the bottom. Further, another edge could exist in the bottom in the form of a fence line, which may or may not prohibit deer travel. Places where several such edges either merge or are close to each other are among the best spots a bowhunter can hang a stand and wait for the buck of his dreams."

Although on-the-ground walking and scouting is the best way to locate edges for deer hunting, Harold says hunters can learn a lot about edges by carefully studying topographic maps of hunting land. Aerial photographs of hunt property also aid sportsmen in getting a fix on edges that may be too large or subtle to notice on the ground while scouting.

Power-line and gas-line right of ways through whitetail woods produce edges deer habitually travel. Often the best places to hunt along such right of ways are in low areas where thick brush flourishes. This situation effectively produces two edges that intersect, making the place a natural for ambushing a buck. Deer walking the right-of-way edge, and whitetails traveling the edge of the low, thick cover, merge, offering a hunter twice the chance of taking an animal moving along an edge.

Sometimes a subtle edge merger can be a superb spot to take a buck, like where a "fire break" intersects an old woods "skid road." Deer walk the fire-break edge, and they also travel the skid road. Hunt near the intersection, and you may bust a buster buck.

A good way to find edge "intersections" is to locate a single edge, says Harold, then walk it scouting for other edges that connect to it.

Maps can be very helpful for bowman looking for terrain edges, such as woods fence lines.

"Say you're walking a field edge and happen upon a fire break that leads into thick woods," he says. "Follow the fire break, and keep a sharp eye out for other edges that merge or occur near the edge you're on, like open grass meadows inside the woods, fence lines, the edge of a grove of crab apple trees, a creek wash, cane thicket, etc.

"It's good to note here that although edges and edge junctures are outstanding places to locate heavily traveled deer trails, don't hunt an edge or an edge junction without abundant deer sign signaling the place is a current hot spot. Emphasize the word current. Old trails, old edges, buck rubs and scrapes may have been good last year or last month. But recent deer droppings, tracks, rubs and scrapes should be the most important considerations in determining how good an edge or edge juncture is for hunting now."

Although almost any field edge, clear-cut edge, power-line right-of-way edge, etc., can be a top spot to bowhunt, according to Harold, frequently "points" or turns on an edge are most often used by deer. For example, in a large field, it's almost a sure bet that a prominent point of woods or "head" will be most attractive to deer moving around and feeding in the area. Also, secluded cuts or back corners in a field edge are favorite spots for whitetails to feed and move around. Some hunters who are also fishermen say this trait is like "structure" to deer.

"It may sound goofy to some people, but deer follow structure in woods and fields almost like bass and crappies migrate along structure in a lake or river," insists Harold, an avid fisherman. "Deer relate to edges—structure, in other words—almost like a bass holds on a creek channel drop-off or a breakline on a submerged point. Like fish, deer use edges to reach their feeding destination, and once there, they scatter. This is like a school of bass holding in deep water, then migrating along a point to a shallow weed bed, then scattering into the weeds to feed. Deer do the same thing when following edges through thick woods into fields for feeding. They stick to edges, then scatter into a food source, usually returning along an edge back to a secure bedding area.

"It took me a while to realize this about deer, but once it sunk in, I started bowhunting 'structure' on field edges, like backfield turns and corners, points, places where old woods roads intersected field corners, anything that looked different or unusual than a straight edge."

Many deer hunters know that big tracts of old pine trees are not particularly appealing to whitetails, since there's not much to eat in mature conifers. However, thick stands of young pines can be superb bedding areas, where choice browsing plants are abundant.

One readily discernible edge well worth hunting, according to Harold, is where young pines (say, less than 10 feet tall) grow beside mature hardwoods or large, mature pines. Such an edge forms a natural connection between feeding and bedding areas. But an edge of this nature diminishes in quality as the trees age.

Young pines growing in a clear-cut area are choice for deer bedding

Bucks often make rubs and "rub lines" along well-defined "edges."

and browsing, and may make for a great hunting edge when they abut an oak ridge. But, again, as pines mature and grow taller, their appeal decreases—particularly for seclusion-seeking mature bucks—as ground cover dies out beneath the spreading canopy of the larger trees.

However, that pine-oak edge may suddenly blossom into a choice spot again if the mature pines are cut and replanted with young pines, once again providing deer with a bedding-browsing area. So the oak-young pine edge is ideal for bowhunting.

It won't come as a surprise to many sportsmen that other game is edge oriented, too. Wild hogs, bears, turkeys, even quail and ruffed grouse, are frequent edge wanderers, since such places offer easy access to dense timber, breeding and nesting areas, and choice feeding sites. Landowners who manage intensely for quail strive to produce edge for bobwhites, which makes ideal cover and food for those birds. Not so coincidentally, quail plantations that have properly managed for bird edge also often have bumper crops of deer and turkeys.

"I love hunting quail, and a lot of plantations that have choice bobwhite hunting are also superb for bowhunting deer—and that's because they have lots of 'edge' cover," explains Harold.

Many types of game-holding edges can be found readily by observant hunters. Edges of creeks, fields, fence lines, tree lines and others can be discovered simply by scouting, and checking maps and aerial photos. But subtle edges, like where pines meet oaks, or a beaver pond abuts a fire break, can only be discovered by hunters willing to walk and scout secluded spots, far from the beaten path.

This "get-off-the-road" approach to locating choice deer-hunting spots has been the hallmark of good hunters, like Harold Knight, for generations. But by watching and searching for edges during scouting trips, odds are good you'll discover whitetail hot spots you likely overlooked in the past. >

Harold Knight is one of the best-known hunters in America. The Cadiz, Kentucky, resident is part of the Knight & Hale Game Call hunting team and an outdoor television show host who has taken countless whitetails throughout America—many of record-book proportions.

Cut-Off Zones

WITH SPENCE PETROS

"Put a bow stand in an area to 'cut off' traveling bucks."

S pence Petros has a friend who owns a northern Illinois duck-hunting lake—one of the best in the state for consistently producing limit bags of mallards. It also forms one of the most remarkable bowhunting spots he's ever seen for giant whitetails.

The lake is big and wide, formed by a half-mile-long earthen dam in a shallow, heavily timbered valley. Below the dam, along the creek forming the lake, it's a network of briers and tangles, as thick as Cambodian jungle. Impenetrable—just the way bucks love it for bedding and resting away from man and predators.

A fence can form a deer barrier. Find a spot where whitetails cross the fence (hole, downed wire, gate, or woods lane), and you may have located a choice cut-off zone for a bruiser buck.

On either side of the lake, above the creek, dam and thicket, are large cornfields in which deer regularly feed. The lake creates a huge barrier, forcing deer in the thickets to walk around the dam and into the corn.

By setting tree stands on either side of the dam, a bowhunter can effectively "cut off" any buck working out of the thicket and into the corn. Spence alternates hunting the two stands, picking whichever is best for wind direction. Over the years, he has bowhunted the lake site four times. He's never needed to hunt it more than three days to arrow a good buck. And he's seen bucks there big enough to get anyone's attention, including a pair of animals he is certain were in the Boone & Crockett class.

Spence says such great hunting spots are not found every day; having a place with such remarkable whitetails that can be "cut off" as well is even more rare. But if more bowhunters spent more time carefully looking and analyzing their hunting terrain, Spence is convinced they'd quickly discover there are many such cut-off spots that can greatly increase odds for whitetail-bowhunting success.

For example, most bowhunters know whitetails regularly travel between feeding and bedding areas. Deer make their moves a time or two each day, and many bucks are arrowed by archers who hunt along such travel areas. The trouble with this hunting tactic, Spence explains, is that all too often, deer utilize so many trails between bedding and feeding areas, they're too scattered to offer consistent bowhunting opportunities. The odds of a good buck wandering by within bow range aren't as high as they could be if a hunter located a concentrated spot to cut off deer. While it's true that such places aren't always available, if you know what you're looking for, they're easier to identify when you see them, contends Spence.

"Figure where deer are feeding, learn where they're bedding," Spence says. "Now locate a place to cut off the bulk of them from a tree stand. Last year, for example, I discovered a very deep, 'wash-out' creek in a draw between a pair of oak ridges that deer were just hammering. The ridges were open, and it seemed like every oak was dropping acorns, so deer weren't concentrated enough to make bowhunting around a single oak very promising. But the creek between the two ridges was super deep, a real pain in the neck to cross. It was hands-and-knees work getting down and then up the other side—except for two places where the banks were less steep, and well-worn whitetail trails crossing the two spots showed deer had found them, too.

"It was a perfect cut-off zone, and I hung a stand 20 yards away, downwind of one creek crossing. From my stand, I also could see the second crossing about 70 yards away. I wanted to put my stand between the two crossings, but the wind was wrong, and I couldn't 'cover' them properly from one stand anyway."

Deep ditches inhibit deer travel patterns. Look for places in such ditches where whitetails cross most easily.

His second morning in the creek-crossing stand, Spence saw a high-rack eight-pointer cross the distant spot, and he passed a pair of 18-month-old bucks that walked over the creek near his stand. A bit after 9 a.m., though, on that frosty morning, a wide nine-pointer showed up, and Spence took him broadside as he slipped across the creek just 18 yards from the archer's tree. Spence had effectively cut off the buck's travel route from one oak ridge to another, and the deer paid the ultimate price.

It's important to concentrate bowhunting efforts on deer-travel patterns according to the way animals are acting at a particular time. The important thing, believes Spence, is the current pattern, because whitetails regularly change their habits—sometimes from week to week.

At times animals move into areas to feed on acorns or apples. Other times they may work corn or soybean field edges. They may go to water, or walk ridges during the rut. Once Spence figures the current deer travel pattern, he goes into the area and looks for a natural barrier that prohibits their free movement to the place they want to go.

"I don't look for tracks or trails, rubs or scrapes," he explains. "What I want to find is a small lake or pond in the woods, 'down' timber, felled trees, a fence, deep ditch, or thick brush—anything that inhibits ease of deer travel through an area. Once I find such a barrier, I place my stand near it—knowing deer will walk around the barrier and I'll cut them off when they come within range. I hunt this way a great deal, and it works well."

Spence hunts one piece of property where there's a long, wide gas-pipe-line right of way. It's a great spot to rifle hunt, but he'd always thought it wasn't worth much for bowhunting because he believed deer could cross the open, 50-yard wide grassy pipeline anywhere. But he was wrong.

One morning while checking the gas line from his ATV, Spence spotted a dozen deer cross the open ground in a spot that pretty much looked like all the other places along the pipeline. Later that morning, he checked the place closely and discovered deer were moving from a thick bottom on one side of the pipeline to a hardwood oak ridge on the other. But they crossed at a very specific spot, because when the gas company cut the timber to make the right of way, they piled up stumps and logs, and used heavy equipment to push them with piles of dirt to either side of the gas line.

The stumps, logs, and dirt had grown up thick in briers and high dog fennel, so they weren't easy for Spence to see. Deer could pick their way through the stumps and logs almost wherever they wanted. But there was a very well-defined opening in the log piles at a spot along the pipeline—just where Spence had watched deer crossing it.

"I was tempted to hang a bow stand right on the pipeline, but a bit of scouting showed a better place was inside the oak ridge, about 100 yards

Felled trees not only help form cut-off zones for ambushing bucks, but sometimes make good ground blinds.

from the gas-line crossing," he says. "It was a natural cut-off spot, since the wind was ideal, and no less than four deer trails necked down to one deep and well-traveled lane leading to the gas-line crossing. First afternoon, I cut off deer crossing the pipeline, I had seven whitetails walk within bow range, including three small bucks. I zipped a high-rack eight-pointer shortly after dawn the next day."

Cut-off whitetail tactics also work well out West. In the Dakotas, Montana, Wyoming, Colorado, and other Western states with plains and mesas, whitetails usually congregate in the major drainages, where there are large cattle ranches with alfalfa and wheat fields. Not only are there deer in the big river bottoms, they're also in feeder creek draws that course down from high mountains through the plains.

During the archery-only season, most deer living around fields are does and small bucks. But good bucks move to and from fields along major drainages from higher elevations. A buck can move a mile or two through a major drainage for feeding with little effort, Spence explains, which is difficult for some Eastern whitetail hunters to comprehend. Stands overlooking such Western draws are outstanding places to cut off bucks moving to and from those alfalfa and wheat fields.

Some of the most productive cut-off spots Spence hunts are found on big river-island points or "necks" leading to grain crop fields. The islands are thick with willows, briers, and impenetrable cover where deer bed, moving to adjacent river-bottom fields at dawn and dusk. It's trail hunting, and key spots are where one island necks down, leading to another island or to a river mainland shore. Deer traffic is heavy between islands, which serve as bedding areas, and mainland fields. Sometimes there are several well-used trails coming off islands onto shore and into fields. Picking the right trail to hunt can be a challenge. But Spence improves his odds by piling thick brush on a trail or two; the blockage directs deer to use the trail he's hunting over—an often deadly tactic.

Spence once used the same type of hunting technique on an eight-foot-high chain-link fence. It was on a military installation, and when he first hunted the place, he found a single hole large enough for deer to slip through the barrier. The fence was several miles long, and except for a couple of main roads, the hole was the only place where whitetails could get through.

In each of the three seasons he hunted the fence hole, Spence arrowed heavy-beam bucks. But when he scouted the fence the fourth year, he found three other large holes. Small animals had burrowed under two places along the fence, giving deer ways to cross the wire.

A third pathway for deer was made when a huge oak fell onto the fence. Spence used boulders and rocks to fill the two holes animals had made, then piled brush and logs to fill the gap at the oak tree. That left only his original hole for deer to get through the fence, which increased whitetail traffic. He arrowed a nice six-pointer the first time he sat in the stand over the spot.

"You've got to be alert to hunt cut-off zones in thickets where you can't see far, because a buck can get past your shooting lanes in thickets at close range very quickly," Spence explains. "You've got to be mentally and physically alert all the time while on a cut-off stand in thick cover."

It seems like the wind blows all the time in some cut-off zones where giant bucks are found, and bowmen must use the wind to their best advantage. Mature bucks are so "wind oriented," it's smart to have four or five stands in a cut-off zone hunting area so you can work a prime spot no matter what direction the wind is blowing.

Never hunt a place when the wind is blowing toward an area you expect deer to approach. Not only will deer spook and remain out of bow range on that particular day, but old, wise, big bucks learn humans are in the cut-off area and that may alter their travel patterns for many days, making the ambush unproductive.

Cut-off zones are great places to collect big bucks, but Spence cautions never to forget that a wise whitetail didn't get old by being stupid. Plan your cut-off zone strategy carefully, and bowhunt the spot intelligently, never tapping the place when conditions are unfavorable. Time and patience in a cut-off zone are your biggest allies. >

Spence Petros, of McHenry, Illinois, is a well-known lifelong Midwest outdoorsman with over 40 years whitetail-hunting experience. He's collected dozens of big Midwest whitetails, including five bucks scoring from 155 to 170 inches.

Creek-Bottom Travel Corridors

WITH STAN POTTS

" The rut had kicked in, and Illinois bowhunter Stan Potts got a call from a pal saying the buck he was hunting was on the move. "

Stan Potts is a low-key bowhunter with a high success rate on giant whitetail bucks. So when he and his wife Brenda walked in to a low brushy creek draw late one summer afternoon while scouting a south-central Illinois farm for the first time, Stan's eyes grew wide, and he stammered with enthusiasm.

"It was a perfect setup for busting a big buck with a bow when the rut kicked in," Stan says. "The farm hadn't been hunted in five years. The landowner only allowed his son to tag a single buck off the spot in all that time. I knew the place would hold some great animals, but I was amazed at what my wife and I discovered when we scouted it that first time."

Stan headed to creek bottoms because they're grown up in timber, brush, briers and brambles, and serve as highways for farm-country bucks. High-ground property is usually planted in corn or soybeans, and when agriculture fields are cut at harvest time, deer stick to the remaining creek-bottom cover.

"I've hunted places like that for years," says Stan. "But this farm had an even better 'funnel' than the usual creeks and draws. On one corner of high ground there was a sporting-clays range. The shooting and human activity there didn't really bother deer. But it forced them to walk around the range, which meant they used two creek draws that crossed just below [southwest] of the range. I used the range as my access or walk-in spot to a stand site I placed along the creek, where several trails crossed. With a south wind, I knew it was just one of those spots that bucks would use when the rut started as they searched for does."

Like many places in Midwest farm country, lowland creek draws having cover and timber are natural travel corridors for bucks in search of does. Stan was certain the spot would produce rutting bucks, and he got even more excited when he checked the place early in bow season and discovered monster-size rubs along the trail where his stand was set. Then the land-

Stan likes creek bottoms because they're grown up in timber, brush, briers and brambles, and serve as highways for farm-country bucks.

owner told Stan he'd seen a huge non-typical buck on the property, and Stan figured he'd found the buck's hideout.

But as the early November rut approached, Illinois' weather was warm, so Stan made a bowhunting trip north to Wisconsin, trying to find rutting bucks in cooler weather. He and his video cameraman Pat Reeve were hunting the Badger State when Stan got a call from his friend Greg Miller, who was hunting the Illinois farm several hundred yards away from Stan's sporting-clays spot.

"On Greg's last day hunting the Illinois farm, he spotted an enormous non-typical buck with a big drop tine, and the buck went into the draw where my stand was hanging," Stan remembers. "He called me in Wisconsin and said that buck had to have walked right by my stand. He

Early in bow season, checthe banks and edges of creeks for deer sign like buck scrapes. These natural drawsare often hot spots when the rut kicks in.

said the Illinois weather was improving and the rut was kicking in.

"That night Pat Reeve and I left Wisconsin for Illinois."

On November 9, the second day back in Illinois, Stan and Pat were in another tree stand. The wind was wrong for them to hunt the spot where Stan wanted to go. But at 6:30 a.m., right at daylight, the wind shifted out of the south, and Stan made the decision to move to the hot spot near the sporting-clays range.

"We got into the stand about 7 a.m., and conditions were perfect," he recalls. "There was a light south wind, temperature about 35 degrees. Soon after we got on stand, a doe and two yearlings came along the trail I was hunting, moving east to west. She was grunting like a buck, and it was pretty amazing listening to her. She moved off along the trail and disappeared into the creek. Not much happened until 9 a.m., when I saw a buck across the creek, and watched him slowly move south.

"I was watching him through my binoculars when I caught some movement of a deer coming off the bean field west of me, down the hill and into the creek draw."

Stan trained his optics on the buck, and instantly saw the huge rack and distinctive drop tine. He alerted the cameraman that a giant buck was coming their way, then watched the buck work a scrape. Stan stood as the buck left the scrape and continued east, along a trail in the creek bottom that would bring him into bow range.

"I could tell by his body language that he wasn't going to stop and feed—just keep on truckin' as he searched for does," explains Stan. "So when he was still a pretty good way out, I drew my bow, and waited for

Stan gets excited about a creek draw when he checks the place and discovers monster-size rubs along trails where his stand is set.

him to step into my shooting lane. As he got to that spot, I mouth-grunted to stop him, and he turned facing me as he looked for the source of the grunt.

"That's a terrible angle, but I could see he was getting more nervous by the second. He was stiffening, and I just knew he was ready to run. He was only 15 yards away, and I felt real confident with the shot, so I took it. My arrow hit him perfectly, just below the white throat patch."

The 100-grain, three-blade Muzzy broadhead on a Beman Hunter carbon shaft buried deep, driven fast by 70 pounds of bow. The buck spun around and dashed along the trail he'd walked in on, up the far hillside, and into the bean field across the draw.

Pat videoed the entire event. They felt the shot had been perfect, and there was plenty of tracking blood on the ground, but the experienced bowmen decided to wait a couple of hours, have lunch, then take up the trail.

Later, a good blood trail led them to the buck, which had crossed the bean field and died in a ditch, 300 yards from where the arrow had hit him.

The estimated five- to six-year-old buck weighed 240-pounds (field dressed), and had 16 non-typical points, including the distinctive drop-tine. It gross scored 221 inches, netting 213 inches, easily making Boone & Crockett, and is one of the largest wild whitetails ever video-recorded taken by bow and arrow.

"It was a great hunt, for a great buck," Stan remembers. "The farm was a perfect spot to bowhunt because the creek bottom travel corridor concentrated its deer, and made it possible for me to get close for a lethal shot." >

Stan Potts of Springfield, Illinois, spends the bulk of his autumns in tree stands chasing monster Midwest deer. He's arrowed better than 20 bucks that would make Pope & Young, and he's taken three bucks gross-scoring over 200 antler inches—arrowed deer that would make the Boone & Crockett record book.

Hunting Saddles for Big Bucks

WITH RALPH CIANCIARULO

"Find a low crossover or gap in a ridge, and you may have located the best spot to bushwhack a buck."

It had been hard bowhunting with a friend in north central Wisconsin, but Ralph Cianciarulo and his partner finally found what they were looking for: They'd discovered a low pass, or "saddle," across a ridge that connected two river draws, and the place had unbelievable deer sign.

"It still ranks as one of the most heavily used deer traffic areas I've ever seen," says Ralph. "Trails from a half-dozen directions out of the draw led to the ridge saddle, narrowing to a pair of trails holding so many tracks, individual hoof prints were almost indiscernible.

"The saddle was thick in briers and low brush, with some head-high trees—a perfect buck funnel. The gap or saddle was maybe 60 yards wide, with steep side hills leading up to the main ridge tops. The two trails were near the saddle center, close together. Mature hardwoods on the ridges above the saddle were perfect for placing stands, offering easy shots through 'holes' in the thickets. The gap traversed the ridge for several hundred yards, and as luck would have it, the wind was ideal. So I could hunt one side of the saddle, my friend could hunt the other side."

The bowmen hung stands on either side of the pass that afternoon, and hunted it. Before dark, they both saw plenty of deer, including several small bucks. But neither drew his bow.

"It was only a weekend trip, so we only had one more day to bowhunt the saddle," recalls Ralph. "My friend was steadfast in holding out for a monster buck, which we found sign from. But I already decided that the first good buck I saw, I'd shoot.

"I'd only been in my tree stand 30 minutes that last afternoon and I started seeing deer, mostly does and yearlings. But finally a small six-pointer showed, and it was all I could do not to pop him. I let him walk through the gap, though, and 45 minutes later was convinced I'd let the buck of my trip go, when a better eight-pointer showed in the tangles, walking down from the ridge into the draw below me. The 12-yard shot was a 'gimme,' and I watched the deer fall within 70 steps of where I'd hit him through the rib cage. My hunt was over and I was ecstatic, quickly gathering my gear and dropping it to the ground."

Within 20 minutes of shooting the buck, Ralph had his sleeves rolled up and started field dressing his deer.

"I don't know what made me look up, but I did, back up toward the ridge saddle," Ralph remembers. "There, moving through the gap, right under the tree where I had been hunting, was a huge buck, something on the order of a 150-inch, 10-pointer. At the time, it was the biggest deer I'd ever seen, and I was sick I hadn't held out on the smaller bucks and waited for the big one. But the eight-pointer I was field dressing was still the best buck I'd yet arrowed. And I remember thinking that the 10-pointer was headed through the gap where my friend was waiting, on the other side of the ridge."

Ralph's buddy saw the buck coming well before he reached bow range. He was ready, and the deer never detected him, at least until he shot. A vine that the bowman hadn't seen deflected the shaft, and the arrow sailed harmlessly over the buck's back.

"We never saw that buck again, not that season, and not during other years we hunted that Wisconsin ridge saddle," says Ralph. "But though that memory is painful for us, learning about how important ridge saddles or gaps are to the movement of whitetails has filled a lot of deer tags for me over the 20 deer seasons that have since passed."

The obvious reason deer (as well as people and other game) funnel through gaps, or saddles, is simply because it's easier to cross a ridge in a spot where terrain definition is not so steep or severe, explains Ralph. This is most notable in big ridge or mountain country, like the Rocky Mountains and, in the East, along the Appalachians. But in almost every state, there are ridges plenty steep to affect game movement.

Even in famously flat places like Illinois and Iowa, South Carolina and Texas there are ridges that interfere enough with game activity that deer, as well as wild hogs and black bears, prefer to keep to low-cut passes. River country in otherwise flat states commonly has steep ridges, formed from erosion. Along the Rock River in north-central Illinois, and along the Illinois and Mississippi rivers, "saddles" can offer red-hot deer-traffic hunting spots in the Land of Lincoln.

"One of the biggest Illinois bucks I ever saw—but, again, didn't get a shot at—ducked into a ridge saddle leading up to a big cornfield off the Rock River near the town of Dixon," Ralph remembers. "Deer were traveling the bottom, but moved up to feed in farm fields on plateaus above the river. I was scouting the river bottom when I saw the buck heading up through the saddle in the ridge. I didn't get him, but I shot the heaviest six-pointer I've ever tagged in that spot the next afternoon."

Generally speaking, the steeper and longer the ridge, the better a saddle will be if you find one cutting through the game-travel barrier, Ralph believes. Deer typically walk a ridge base, parallel to it, looking for an easy way to cross. If the ridge is a mile or two long, then suddenly opens into a gap, with the ridge again rising on the other side of the gap, it's likely you've discovered a gold mine of a deer-stand site. For this reason, too, the steeper the ridge barrier, the more likely deer are to funnel through any pass that's easy to traverse.

"It's important that a saddle or gap leads to an area desirable to deer," Ralph emphasizes. "If another tangled draw or agricultural fields are accessible through a gap, the place should be tops. If a four-lane highway is adjacent to the gap, it's unlikely deer use the saddle much. Just read the deer sign in the gap, and that should tell a bowhunter everything he needs to know about how good a spot it is."

Ralph says sometimes several ridges taper down into a low spot from several directions, forming a kind of natural collecting spot of gaps or saddles. The ridges often diminish at their ends into a creek drain or "bowl." Deer usually walk the low creek draws, and the natural way for them to traverse from one draw to the next is to work to the end of a ridge, where it forms a gap, which in this case collects into a bowl or basin where several tapering ridges meet.

"I once hunted such a secluded saddle hot spot in rolling Kentucky hills, not far from Cincinnati, that had six different ridges collecting into a single bowl," Ralph relates. "It was, in effect, a 'pass' for traveling game along three distinct ridges. The place was a great spot for deer any time weather and wind

One of the great things about "saddle bowhunting," says Ralph, is you can scout a spot without ever seeing the place with the simple use of topographic and/or aerial survey maps.

conditions were good. But it shone brightest on opening week of rifle season, when the hills were crawling with orange-clad deer hunters. Opening day was a sure thing for collecting a buck with a bow there, and only a fool would shoot a deer having less than eight points. I never hunted the place except with a bow, and it was best during opening week of gun season—even if I had to wear blaze-orange outer garments."

One of the great things about "saddle bowhunting," says Ralph, is you can scout a spot without ever seeing the place with the simple use of topographic and/or aerial survey maps. This is extremely valuable for weekend jaunts to distant unfamiliar spots, or for limited-duration "drawn" hunts on

While saddle hunting is often one of the fastest ways to tag a buck in many areas, it's important to let available deer sign determine whether the spot is worth hunting.

military or WMA lands, where scouting and hunting time is at a premium—especially when they're a long drive from home.

On topo maps, Ralph suggests looking for four to eight "relief lines" that are very close together, which indicates steep terrain. Next, find a place (river and stream areas are especially good, particularly in otherwise flatland country) where close relief lines extend for a long distance. A mile or so is ideal.

Now, carefully study the lines and look for any place where they suddenly widen. This indicates the ridge diminishes in steepness, forming a "pass." If the contour lines show there is a saddle or gap that extends completely through the ridge, the place is worth scouting carefully. By locating several such places on topo maps, scouting can be done very quickly on land you've not previously seen.

While saddle hunting is often one of the fastest means to tagging a buck in many areas, it's important to let available deer sign determine whether the spot is worth hunting.

"If there are no trails, or if trails are not heavily used, don't waste your time there," advises Ralph. "Log the spot, and check it periodically, because deer travel corridors change with the seasons, weather, and availability of food and cover. A saddle in September might not be worth hunting. But in December, it may be the most choice spot in the area to arrow a buster buck." >

Ralph Cianciarulo is host of Archer's Choice television show and videos. He travels extensively, bowhunting with his wife, Vicki. This Illinois archer still ranks the whitetail as his favorite bow target. He took his first deer with a bow at age 14, and has since collected hundreds of whitetails using archery gear, including two Boone & Crockett bucks. His best is a 188⅞-inch monster from Kansas.

Urban Whitetails, City Slickers

WITH DAVID BLANTON

"Ever thought of heading into town for hunting deer?"

I t was cool by October middle-Georgia standards, and dark as it only can be driving in the rural deep South at 4 a.m. But suddenly town lights appeared, farmhouses were replaced by city street lamps, traffic signals and an occasional passing automobile.

"Where are we going?" a companion asked David Blanton, of RealTree Camouflage television fame.

"We're going bowhunting," he snickered. "And I'm taking you to the best deer spot in all of west-central Georgia."

His friend countered sarcastically as they pulled in for a fast-food breakfast and coffee, "Sure, and where is this great spot—beside the Burger King?"

"No, of course not," David replied smiling. "It's a block over, next to the university campus."

David wasn't kidding. The place was just 300 yards from pretty coeds walking to class. It was surrounded by upscale subdivisions. In fact, from David's tree stand he could see a sprawling country mansion, and watch a beautiful tall blonde woman play catch with a black Labrador retriever—the same stand where, in three days bowhunting, he saw seven good bucks and arrowed two deer.

The hunt property was a 1,000-acre privately owned deer haven, where the large Southern town and college campus had grown. The place was jammed with whitetails, and there were some monster bucks because the age structure of animals was so outstanding. The buck-doe ratio was kept carefully in balance by the landowner and David, because no outsiders were allowed on the place and no firearms were legal inside city limits.

It was the ultimate whitetail bowhunting paradise.

It not only had plenty of deer, but there were Boone & Crockett candidates, some of which had been featured in one of the first RealTree videos to show outsize bucks still in velvet feeding in a sprawling green kudzu patch.

If you've ever watched that video, you've seen the kind of bowhunting you can experience by driving into town, not out of it, in some of today's urban whitetail country. And it's happening all across the U.S.; in fact it's even more prevalent in some of the largest sprawling metro areas of the

As suburbia sprawls, deer have learned to thrive beside human development. Bowhunting opportunities abound in such places.

nation.

"Deer have learned to thrive in human habitat," says David, a wildlife biologist by education. "As cities and subdivisions spread into ever-more-rural areas, deer aren't displaced, they're simply absorbed into the country lifestyle of people trying to escape the hectic concrete world of cities. With no predators, plenty to eat, and generally no firearms hunting, deer have proliferated, and bucks have grown to record-book size."

Ten years ago this sort of urban sprawl usually meant posting "No Hunting or Trespassing" signs in traditional whitetail spots. But even office-tower yuppies with no love for hunters are learning that too many deer living on their well-manicured rural estates are not only bad for petunias, apple trees and tomato plants, but the odds for BMW-whitetail collisions have increased significantly.

David says the result of this interesting turn of hunting events is a windfall for some bowhunters, like those who live in and near the Twin Cities of Minneapolis-St. Paul, Minnesota. There, hundreds of archers belong to the "Metro Bowhunter Resource Base (MBRB)," which, through a cooperative effort with the cities, surrounding suburban communities, police and the state DNR, are allowed to bowhunt whitetails in areas where firearms hunting is not permitted.

Bowmen who join the MBRB (non-residents are invited, too) must take a 10-hour-long bowhunter-education class, pass a bowhunting proficiency test and pay a small fee to be eligible for permit drawings for special Twin Cities hunts. Some bowhunts are conducted on city parks, others are held in small suburban communities where deer have become such a nuisance that homeowners contact the municipalities, which contact the state DNR, which in turn calls the MBRB.

The results are outstanding. One year, no less than two Pope & Young bucks were arrowed on Twin Cities urban deer land, including a 147⅛-point buck taken by Marlene Odahlen/Hinz while bowhunting a private 62-acre subdivision whose homeowners contacted the MBRB to reduce the burgeoning deer herd.

A second Pope & Young (P&Y) buck was taken by a bowhunter at Lebanon Hills Park. Management rules on the park require bowhunters to harvest a doe before they shoot a buck, and the fortunate bowman who got the P&Y buck saw the deer one day but couldn't shoot it because he hadn't yet taken a doe. He moved to another site, shot a doe with his bow, returned to where he saw the record-book buck, and arrowed it.

The MBRB has been operational for years and works well. They have a hotline phone number bowhunters call to learn what hunts are available, and they can see how many permits are remaining for each hunt. Most years the group has over a dozen bowhunts, and they're very effective at keeping urban deer herds in check in places where firearms are not practical. In addition, hunts are cost-effective for areas that may be considering hiring a "sharpshooter" to come in and reduce a deer herd.

A sharpshooter was going to be hired to take 50 deer off the Twin Cities Arsenal, a fenced two-square-mile site—until they contacted the MBRB. Bowhunters went in instead and took 69 whitetails out the first year. Now the Arsenal is managed by bowmen who keep the deer herd in check while also providing safe outdoor recreation for many sportsmen.

It's common to find big-rack whitetails near suburban estates in many regions.

The MBRB has been so successful in the Twin Cities that other metro areas with deer-control problems, like Detroit, have sought their assistance in setting up similar programs. Still, anti-hunters and some city councils don't always understand the viability of archery for deer control, or the need for such urban outdoor recreation. Often, big cities with big deer-herd problems completely avoid the issue.

"Obviously, much of the very best urban bow deer hunting is available on private land," David continues. "And while such property usually is locked up tight, there are signs in some whitetail areas that landowners are beginning to welcome hunters—especially bowhunters—with new-found respect."

The ritzy town of Fox Chapel, near Pittsburgh, had such a problem with deer that they had the local police department find bowhunters who were courteous and qualified to thin the herd. It worked so perfectly that well-heeled suburban estate owners became very friendly with the bow-hunters and learned to greatly respect their skills. Some went out of their

Golf courses in large suburban settings are often jammed with whitetails, and some allow bowhunting.

way to introduce archers to other nearby landowners. They were proud of the fact they had their own bowhunter to manage their estate deer herd, almost like old English land barons who had their own gamekeepers.

Also in Pennsylvania, the Philadelphia area generally disallows the use of firearms, so the surrounding counties of Chester, Delaware, and Bucks have the highest number of deer per square mile of forestland in the state. Huge bucks are available to bowhunters in those counties because of the improved age class, so record-size animals are taken regularly. Two state-record typical-rack bow-harvested Pennsylvania bucks have come from areas near Philadelphia, including the current 175⅝-inch record-book buck that was arrowed less than 60 miles from the city.

Allegheny County, which includes Pittsburgh, has a lot more wooded areas than Philadelphia, and only one public hunting area. Yet that county has more "book bucks" than any other in the state, with some of the biggest deer available near the Pittsburgh Airport.

Golf-course communities in large suburban settings are often jammed with whitetails—so much so that greens keepers and landscapers have difficult times keeping the greens green and the flowers blooming around otherwise well-maintained clubhouses. Many P&Y bucks are arrowed in woodlots bordering urban golf courses, and often crews in charge of the links are only too happy to see the whitetail herd thinned. Getting the okay to bowhunt from a golf club, or homeowner on the club, isn't nearly as difficult as one might believe, especially during late autumn and winter, when golfers are huddled closer to the fire than a sand trap.

One Virginia bowman hunts near the golf links beside a large country club home owned by a pal's grandmother. His favorite tree stand is within sight of the home, and the elderly lady waves to him each morning shortly after sunrise.

"She gets a kick out of seeing me in that tree stand while drinking her morning tea, and gets more excited than I do when I stand, take a shot, and arrow a deer," says the golf-links bowhunter. "Twice I've shot a buck,

Some great bucks are arrowed even in city limits.

looked over toward her house, and she was giving me the 'thumbs-up' sign, knowing I've taken a deer. She still likes seeing whitetails around her home and golf course, but she couldn't grow flowers in her garden. First year there, she was so glad I was hunting deer, she brought hot tea and homemade cookies out to my stand. I was going to explain to her why that wasn't such a good idea, but then I figured the deer were used to her. So I kept my mouth shut.

"Hasn't seemed to hurt much. I took a nine-point buck there last November, during the rut, and it scored nearly big enough for the record book."

Similar urban-bowhunting stories abound in the counties surrounding deer-rich and sprawling Atlanta—Cobb, DeKalb, Clayton, and part of Fulton—according to David. Some of the most successful bowhunters in the area are construction workers. Pushing over 10-, 50-, 100-acre tracts of woods all day, hammering nails in new houses and building suburban roads, they're outside all the time, and they see deer constantly in those new development areas, so they know where the better bucks live. A lot of construction workers knock off an hour or so early in fall, or get to a building site a little early, and arrow deer no other hunter has even a clue are living in the area.

There are huge bucks all over the wooded metro Atlanta area because there's no gun hunting allowed. One Georgia bowhunter there one fall saw a huge eight-pointer near his house in DeKalb County, and says the buck would have scored 140-points, easily making P&Y. The rut was in swing and the buck was standing in the wide open between a church and a grocery store.

Another Atlanta area hunter swears he knows where the best stand is located in all of Cobb County: on top of a tall playground slide in a sprawling green park bordering a small 10-acre woodlot. Every year during the rut, he sees giant-rack bucks there, and somehow he knows they walk within bow range of that park slide.

Similar tales about urban whitetails can be heard throughout prime urban deer country, in places like Trenton, New Jersey; Buffalo, New York; Richmond, Virginia; Kansas City, St. Louis, Des Moines, Chicago, Milwaukee, Raleigh, Charlotte, Baltimore, and Washington, D.C.

One of the best spots for buster urban bucks in America is around Charleston, West Virginia, where four counties are only open to archery deer hunting. Some of the state's biggest bucks are found there because there are more three-and-a-half to six-and-a-half-year-old whitetails than in other regions. Bow-only counties include Wyoming, Logan, Mingo, and McDowell, and they produce some record-book animals every year. Two of the best include a typical whitetail that scored 168⅝ points, taken from Wyoming County, and a non-typical buck scoring 189⅛-points from McDowell County.

While getting a buck of such size is every bowhunter's goal, it's not realistic in every bow-only urban hunting region. Still, the hunting is great and access is easier than one might at first believe.

One Wisconsin bowhunter relates the story of a girlfriend telling him about a neighbor outside Milwaukee who was having trouble from "deer pests." The guy didn't think much about it, but one of the "pests" she described was a heavy-beam 10-pointer she saw one night in that same neighbor's front yard.

The next day, the bowhunter went to the lady's house, knocked on her door, and when she opened it, he asked if she was the person having trouble with deer pests.

"Why, yes," she replied excitedly. "Those deer are terribly destructive. They really are an awful nuisance."

"Well, ma'am," he replied smiling, holding his hat in his hands. "I'm the exterminator and I'm here to solve your whitetail pest problem with my bow and arrows." >

David Blanton of RealTree *television lives in Georgia and has taken well over 100 whitetails with a bow, including several large record-book bucks.*

Picture This!

WITH STACER HELTON

"*Placing remote cameras in the woods to record game activity can aid bowhunters.*"

Dedicated whitetail hunter Stacer Helton of Sandersville, Georgia, knew his deer lease was a good one. But it was large, and he couldn't monitor his dozen stands on a regular daily basis. When he made hunts to the lease, he could only spend a few hours each day in a stand that he believed offered the best opportunity for a buck.

Thus Stacer did what many serious bowhunters do—started second-guessing himself each time he sat in a tree stand. He'd think about another spot, then wonder if he should be hunting that place instead of the one he'd chosen.

"It was a mind game that drove me crazy, and it got worse each time I found fresh rubs, scrapes or tracks at a spot I hadn't chosen to hunt," he explained. "My confidence level dropped to almost zero on many of the places I picked to hunt. And when I did feel good about a spot, from sign I found, I'd often bowhunt it and not see the kind of animals I believed were using the area.

"It was driving me nuts, because I obviously couldn't be in two stands at the same time."

Then Stacer saw an advertisement for an automatic game monitor rigged to a camera that photographed animals as

Trail cameras placed in likely deer areas can reveal many things that bowmen otherwise may not see.

103

they wandered through an area. He recognized immediately that such a system would solve many of his hunting hassles, so he bought one of the special cameras and tried it.

The first unit he tested was inexpensive, and not very reliable. But the photos it produced around his lease food plots and tree stands were so remarkable, he quickly upgraded to a more expensive but better, dependable camera—with startling results.

"I had a small food plot in thick pines on my lease that had a lot of fresh deer sign, so I set up a stand and put my remote camera on the tree a month before the opening of bow season," he says. "The unit cost nearly $400. But it was a good-quality camera, completely waterproof, and had a strong money-back guarantee. I figured I had everything to gain, so I tried it. I left it for a week and came back, and the whole roll of 36-exposure 35mm film was shot.

"I got 'em developed in an hour, and I couldn't believe what was going on at the food plot when I wasn't there."

The camera recorded the time and date each photo was made, so Stacer could instantly pattern the animals using his food plot—without overly contaminating the area with human scent. He learned that four different bucks were regularly coming into the plot: two small deer, a large six-pointer, and a heavy-beam, wide-rack eight-point. Stacer ordinarily would have shot the six-pointer with his bow the first time he had the opportunity. But knowing the eight-pointer was using the area, he decided to pass on the smaller buck in hopes of downing the larger animal.

Stacer moved the camera to another stand location a half mile from his food plot, and discovered a heavy-beam seven-point buck was predictably walking along a trail late every day, about 7 p.m. Three evenings in a row, the buck tripped the camera's shutter within minutes of 7 p.m. Three other times, the buck walked passed the camera lens within 30 minutes of 7 p.m. Stacer was confident of taking that buck one late afternoon when the season opened. But the deer suddenly changed its pattern and began moving through the area at night—also recorded by the camera.

"I couldn't figure what made the buck change its timetable, until I looked at my calendar's moon phase chart," Stacer says. "The buck became more nocturnal during the full moon, just like I always believed some mature deer do. It proved to me that moon phase definitely has a bearing on deer activity, and this was even before bow season opened."

Following the full moon, the seven-pointer settled back into his old pattern of walking the trail around 7 p.m., a predictable time for Stacer to place a tree stand ambush for the buck during a dark moon phase.

Something else Stacer learned from the seven-pointer: Big bucks seem unaffected by the flash of a camera at night. They completely ignored the flash, as shown in several photos recorded over nearly a week's span—including three pictures in a single night, when the animal stopped to make a scrape in a trail.

Remote cameras are valuable to bowmen who discover a line of scrapes or rubs. Placing a camera over a scrape or near rubs will not only tell a hunter what size and number bucks are making the sign, but also offers information about when rubs and scrapes are made. The hottest scrape sign in the county will do an archer no good if bucks are only working the site at night.

A great buck may frequent one of your prime hunt areas at times you aren't on stand. Learning this is easy with a quality trail camera.

Once Stacer and his hunting pal Kenny Driggers set out several remote cameras on their central Georgia lease, just as bucks were beginning to scrape. They quickly learned one large scrape along a secluded field edge had a lot of activity. They recorded no less than four different racked bucks hitting the scrape, including a giant eight-point that Kenny shot over the scrape late one afternoon.

"The camera really helped narrow our hunting window," Stacer reports. "We would have spent a lot of time hunting other stands and scrape sites looking for a good buck. And at the scrape where Kenny hunted he may have settled for a smaller deer than the one he shot. Remote cameras are remarkable tools. Something dedicated, serious deer hunters find invaluable."

Remote cameras can also provide poacher and trespass information, if you're having trouble with illegal hunters and trespassers on private land. An automatic camera gives you photographic evidence to help halt the lawbreakers.

Cameras do not spook whitetails—not even their flash at night. CREDIT FIDUCCIA ENTERPRISES.

Improved remote-camera technology in recent years has made them practical and fairly routine for in-the-field use by bowmen. Reliable, high-quality "point-and-shoot" 35mm cameras made by Minolta, Pentax, Olympus, Canon, and other companies have made focusing, automatic film advance and flash synchronization simple. When such a camera is placed in a waterproof, shock-resistant housing, and triggered by a motion- or infra-red-heat sensor, the unit becomes an indispensable source of information for modern hunters.

The newest advance in the remote-camera boom is digital imaging—even digital remote videography. Digital cameras are especially helpful for hunters because they can be checked right at the site, the images viewed instantly. If, for example, the camera records 24 images, the hunter can quickly review the digital pictures and delete those that don't concern him—photos of raccoons, hen turkeys, doe deer, armadillos, etc.

If a few of the images are worth keeping, a hunter can remove that disk and put a fresh one in the camera. When he gets back to his computer, he can download the images on the disk he brought home, view them large size on the computer monitor, save the ones he wants and, perhaps, print them out.

Once images have been downloaded from disk to computer, saved and/ or printed, the disk can be reused. Some digital disks can hold hundreds of color images—something no standard film camera can do. That large recording capacity makes digital cameras especially valuable for hunters who choose not to visit a particular site often, but don't want to miss recording game that may stroll by over a period of time. And some digitals have infrared capability, so they can take photographs of game up to 25 feet away in total darkness.

"My remote camera has become an important hunting partner," Stacer reports happily. "Finally, I've learned how to be in two places at once, or at least have my camera there when I'm not. I always thought it was fun and exciting to pull an exposed roll of film out of my woods camera. Now I can get my woods photos without going to the camera store—pictures of does and nursing fawns, good bucks making rubs and scrapes, and other game, too, like bobcats, coyotes, foxes, and turkeys. I look forward to getting my woods photographs back . . . like a kid waiting for presents at Christmas. It's almost as much fun as actually bowhunting." >

Stacer Helton of Sandersville, Georgia, is a lifelong deer hunter. He has widely traveled hunting experience, and has collected giant bucks from many parts of America and Canada.

PART FOUR

WHITETAIL TACTICS

Early Season Tactics

WITH CHRIS KIRBY

"Deer have home field advantage. So to be consistently successful, you must have a game plan for early season."

U nderstand from the outset that there is no ultimate game plan for an opening day, or weekend, deer bowhunt, says Chris Kirby, head man at Quaker Boy Game Calls in New York. What works for Chris in the western part of his state in October may not work for you on the Upper Peninsula of Michigan; or for others hunting public land in Maryland; or for those on large private ranches in Texas. But that, ironically says Chris, is the basis for the best deer early-season "game plan"—being flexible.

"Like the football coach who has done his homework scouting the opposing team, planning his plays and positioning his players, a deer

bowhunter can do much the same things," says Chris. "But a good, winning football coach also adapts to conditions. If the original game plan isn't working, a smart coach shifts gears, tries other options, probes the defense of the opposition, and capitalizes on those weaknesses. This is why, at half-time, good coaches suddenly can turn a game around from an apparent loss to a decided victory.

"Same is true with an opening weekend deer bowhunt. If the first half of your hunt is a bust, re-group, re-plan, and try alternate hunting sites and/or tactics."

Chris says important factors on where and how a sportsman bow-

Chris says high-traffic deer travel corridors, like creek draws, can really shine for opening-week bowhunts.

hunts for opening-day whitetails include: hunting pressure in the area, private or public land tapped, weather, wind, wet or dry conditions, herd density, and how close to the rut the hunt is timed.

Naturally, scouting and preparation are keys to any early-season deer bowhunt. Chris begins his preparation for opening day in spring, as early as April in New York, in setting up food plots and places bucks will feel secure through spring and summer. By opening day of bow season, Chris knows where 2½- to 3½-year-old bucks will be available to him.

"I love that first week of bow season. So many adult bucks are not spooky because humans haven't been in the woods all year," he declares. "They are easy to pattern and very susceptible to hunting and calling—even though they are a long way from coming into rut.

"Bucks will be feeding on the highest quality food available, and they'll be living close to it. I spend a lot of time hunting downwind around fields because I can see whitetails in the open areas, and if a good buck is working through, I have good success calling him within bow range. A little soft grunting or using a doe bleat will dupe a lot of two- and three-year-old bucks during that first week or two of bowhunting because they don't have a clue hunters are around. They don't come running to calling like they may later during the rut, but they're curious, and unwary, and that makes them very vulnerable to bowhunting."

As an example of how susceptible adult bucks can be, Chris relates the story of a 137-inch nine-pointer he arrowed one opening week of bow season in western New York. He was hunting with his wife, Michelle, and he put her in stands near the edges of cornfields with ripe apple trees nearby. The place was loaded with deer, and several good bucks. No other bowhunters were in the area, and Chris was careful to see that he and Michelle didn't alarm the animals.

They only hunted afternoons, for fear of spooking deer as they approached stands in pre-dawn dark. During a week of bowhunting, Michelle missed the nine-pointer twice, but the buck never knew he was being hunted—until he wandered by Chris' stand.

"Yeah. I shot my wife's buck," Chris admits, smiling. "But, hey, she had two chances, and I knew we needed to get the buck that first week or we'd likely never have a chance at getting him at all. Once other hunters got in the woods, that buck likely would have gone nocturnal, or been shot by someone else."

Chris says it's smart to be on hunt property long before the season opens, looking for tracks, trails, old rubs, and scrapes. Find choice food sources. Walk perimeters of fields. Learn where deer are feeding and bedding, walking, and getting water. You can't spend too much time afield, he insists.

Chris Kirby says it's smart to be on hunt property long before the season opens, looking for tracks, trails, old rubs and scrapes. CREDIT QUAKER BOY GAME CALLS

Late summer and early fall, deer usually are easy to pattern, especially when they haven't been harassed by hunters, says Chris. Most whitetails are feeding in crop fields, around oaks and "soft mast," clear-cuts and thick browse areas early and late in the day. In dry conditions, deer bed around thick draws with water, and they'll visit water holes for drinking. When you're driving a vehicle and glassing with binoculars, such places can quickly pinpoint spots harboring deer, which then must be walked and carefully scrutinized before stands are set. Talk to farmers and friends in rural areas to learn where they're seeing deer, and when, and be sure to ask about bucks.

It's surprising how many large bucks are downed every opening day in places where someone had regularly spotted the deer and reported it to a bowhunter, says Chris, who has a nationwide network of "field staff" bowhunters who also work for Quaker Boy, and keep him informed of such things.

"Timely good buck location information isn't always available, so when it drops in your lap, be sure to take advantage of it," says Chris. "Check out the place where such a buck has been spotted during the 'off' season, because the best chance to collect him is during the opening weeks, before he realizes hunters are on the prowl.

"You might begin a day bowhunting such a known buck at the site where he'd been regularly seen, which frequently is a field corner or field ditch bottleneck. Then, knowing plenty of hunters are afoot, you might

Choose a stand that overlooks a number of different trails in a travel corridor where pre-season scouting has shown plenty of deer activity. CREDIT QUAKER BOY GAME CALLS

move at mid-day to a funnel or neck-down area leading to the closest thicket or potential bedding area.

"Be sure to have several different hunting locations pinpointed, and stands set, at least a week before opening day. If you have only one area to bowhunt, have several different stands hanging in various places, affording good chances to see and tag deer according to wind direction and the 'temperament' of the animals—spooky, calm, in pre-rut, etc.

"I 'grade' the spots I can bowhunt opening weekend, and I only tap the very best locations when conditions are absolutely perfect. Frequently, I hunt the least good spots first, particularly 'peripheral' areas if hunting conditions are less than ideal. It can be wise to save the best interior or 'core' spots for when weather and wind conditions are perfect, especially on large tracts of private land."

However, Chris insists that if you have only a few days to hunt, or if you only have the opening day or two to be in the woods, or if you hunt public ground, by all means, hunt the best spots you know. But be certain your approaches to stands are wise, the wind completely favorable. Chris would rather not hunt the hottest of hot spots if the wind is wrong, when he might stumble in to it and alert bucks he's in their neighborhood. You just might be able to squeeze in another day of hunting later or, perhaps, offer the spot to your best friend or brother when conditions improve, says Chris.

"Keep in mind that opening weekend is a great 'first-strike' opportunity to tag bucks lulled into believing the woods are safe—their sole domain," explains Chris, who is nationally known as a game-calling expert. "An open bean field may never have a daytime mature buck in it after the first week of the season. But opening morning, there could be a 'Booner' standing on the field edge feeding, completely oblivious to the danger soon to be around him."

Chris says high-traffic deer travel corridors, like creek draws and overgrown field fence lines, really can shine opening week, when animals are pushed by hunters on the move. That's particularly true in states where there are a lot of archers, like New York, Michigan, Wisconsin, and Pennsylvania. Choose a stand that overlooks a number of different trails in a travel corridor where pre-season scouting has shown plenty of deer activity. Use quality optics, and stay constantly alert.

Sometimes the best places for opening day bowhunting are on border edges of private land, says Chris. One of the best opening day bow stands he ever had was on a large farm that abutted a public hunting area. The state hunting spot was crawling with archers opening morning. But deer that had been living in the WMA quickly vacated the place, heading to cover in surrounding private land holdings.

Chris hunted the place twice, and both times collected nice bucks by mid-morning. He'd found a fence line separating the WMA from the farm, and there were two overgrown creeks that bisected the fence. Deer traveled the cover of the creeks, crossing the fence to the comparative safety of the private farm. A pair of large trees within easy bow range of both creeks made the spot a choice archery stand.

Often on large tracts of private land, where there's low hunting pressure, deer pushed into core areas from adjacent property go right back into their normal routines. Set stands on oak ridges overlooking trails and draws, check field corners and edges, and be sure to have stands set near food sources.

A good game plan for opening-week bowhunting is to get on stand early near a property "peripheral" area or a "funnel" close to a deer-bedding zone, Chris advises, and to stay on stand as late as possible. Bring a daypack with plenty of food and water, making sure you have the right clothing and accessories to make your stay comfortable.

If you've got to get down and move around, walk at mid-day and do a little slow scouting into the wind. Use binoculars often, says Chris, and get back on stand by early afternoon—perhaps a different spot overlooking a feeding area where you've seen deer.

The next day should be a repeat performance, hopefully on different stands, so as not to "over-hunt" a spot, and to help learn what deer are doing at various places on your hunt property.

"Finally," says Chris, "be positive about hunting opening week. Believe you're going to tag a book buck. Sure it can be hot, and bugs can be awful. But it's one of the best times to be in the woods, because big bucks don't yet understand they're being hunted.

"Stay alert. Start hunting early, quit hunting late. Scout, glass, and don't give up. Not ever. It'll pay off—big time!" >

Chris Kirby is president of Quaker Boy Game Calls in Orchard Park, New York. Although he missed the first 26 deer he bowhunted before taking one with an arrow, he was just 13 when he collected his first bow whitetail. Since then, he's taken countless whitetails from throughout America, including three record-book bucks by bow, and eight large-rack bucks from upstate New York.

Ground-Blind Bucks

WITH CLAUDE POLLINGTON

"Tree stands are great, but sometimes you 'gotta get down' to get deer."

Years ago, before the enlightened age of tree stands, whitetail bow-hunters routinely took game from terra firma. In fact, some of the biggest bucks arrowed by such legendary bowhunters as Fred Bear and Howard Hill, were taken from the ground. Those days, however, are mostly gone for modern whitetail bowmen. Today, it's likely 95 percent of all deer taken by archers are ambushed from the treetops.

Contemporary bowhunters are so habitually tree-stand oriented, that even when a great hunting spot is found, an archer will not even try to take a deer from the place unless there's a tree to accommodate a stand nearby.

That's a major mistake, though, says legendary longtime Michigan bowhunter Claude Pollington. Plenty of prime spots for bushwhacking a buck have no trees suitable for setting stands. Furthermore, in some locales bucks are so accustomed to bowhunters working from treetops, they are less likely to spot a well-made, well-camouflaged ground blind or "pit."

Effective ground blinds can be simple makeshift "hides" constructed from down timber, stumps and treetops. Great blinds also can be made from other materials, including old, heavy-duty Army blankets. You

Complete head-to-toe camouflage clothing is even more important for low-level bowhunters than it is for tree-stand archers.

build a wooden frame, nail olive-drab blankets to it, then cut several one-foot square "shooting ports" out of the fabric at a level equal to a stool sitting position inside the blind. Finally, pile brush and tree limbs around the outside of the blind to make it blend with natural surroundings at the spot you've chosen for your ambush. Pine straw, and the boughs of fir, cedar and pine are especially good for ground-blind camouflage because they are very aromatic, which helps mask human scent.

Claude is expert in building semi-permanent ground blinds from weathered scrap lumber, because it blends well with wooded terrain. In Michigan, where for years it was illegal to hunt deer from tree stands during the firearms season, such wooden ground blinds, affectionately called "coops," are very popular with sportsmen. Positioned on hillsides, field edges, near deer crossings, fire breaks and power lines, well-made coops, are extremely comfortable and provide both overhead cover and warmth against biting Midwest wind, snow and sleet. A good coop has a couple of shooting holes or "slots," but is otherwise solid, so hunter movement is mostly concealed from game.

Most coops on private land are semi-permanent, and in Michigan, hunters are so accustomed and confident hunting from them that during archery season, they use the same ground-level shooting houses—often with remarkable success. Claude has taken countless big bucks from coops with a bow.

"Bowhunters should concentrate building ground blinds in areas where deer are comfortable and at ease with their surroundings," says Claude, who is widely known in his deer-rich state as the "Whitetail Wizard." "Often, the biggest bucks live in the very thickest, heaviest cover. Frequently those places are alder bottoms, marshes, and swamps that have few large trees for stands. This type cover provides protection for deer, and not many hunters—including bowmen—venture into them because there are no places to 'hang' a stand. But building a coop shooting house from weathered lumber well ahead of season in such places can be the ticket to a bowhunter's biggest buck."

Claude notes that when building a coop, it should be wide enough and high enough to allow for plenty of bowhunter movement. Moving around quietly in the closed-in space with an arrow nocked on a bow is not easy, especially when a good buck is nearby. If there's a coop roof, be sure there's ample height for top bow-limb clearance.

A good bowhunting coop has three or four shooting ports, and it's important to make the holes big enough, roughly twelve inches by eight inches. The rectangular holes should give the hunter enough of an opening to properly aim his bow and loose his arrow.

One vital consideration, Claude emphasizes, is that a ground blind must blend in with adjacent terrain features. A good example of this, and of how being adaptable is key to ground-blind deer-hunting success, is this story about Colorado hunting guide Judd Cooney.

Judd was bowhunting with a pal for Alberta's giant bucks, and they located two Boone & Crockett animals that seemed impossible to ambush. The deer emerged every afternoon from a small strip of woods and walked into a cut hay field to feed. Prevailing wind was such that no approach

Small "shooting holes" are best for ground blinds.

could be made to the spot to hunt in the woods. A standard ground blind would have stood out like an oak in the Sahara because of the close-cropped hay field.

But a farmer had rolled the cut hay into huge bales, and that gave Judd the idea of making a ground blind the same size, shape, and color as the bales. He constructed a round frame with chicken wire and wove hay into the frame so it looked exactly like a real bale—except it was hollow inside, with plenty of space for Judd's bowhunting buddy.

They positioned the fake bale near the woods strip and gave the bucks several days to get used to it. The first afternoon Judd's pal occupied the hollow bale blind, he arrowed one of the massive bucks; its rack easily scored big enough to make the Boone & Crockett books.

A pit blind is another exceptional way to disappear from a deer's watchful eyes, and it's become one of Claude's favorite whitetail hunting sites. A pit can be beneficial because it helps contain hunter scent. The rigorous labor required to dig a human-size hole in rocky or frozen ground may temper your passion for whitetail bowhunting, or at least this method. Still, at times nothing is better than a pit to bushwhack a buck.

While the best pits are deep and roomy, even ones that are just knee-high help conceal a hunter from wary bucks. Such a shallow hole allows a bowman to at least sit down on the pit rim, which can be quite comfortable, particularly if a camouflage cushion is used as a seat. Comfort is something ground-blind hunters never should overlook when long hours of still, silent waiting are on tap, says Claude, since the slightest movement can be spotted instantly by a wary whitetail.

"Be sure to ring the top of a pit opening with brush, tree limbs or corn stalks to conceal your head when peering out of a foxhole," advises Claude. "But make sure such cover is far enough away from you in a pit to allow quiet bow movement. Opening a few 'holes' or ports in natural cover is the ideal way of concealing bowhunter movement during shooting. This is much better than having to come up-and-over brush or tree limbs, or leaving wide 'lanes' in cover through which to shoot. A hole with a top, bottom, and sides of brush and limbs offers the most concealment to an archer while still allowing an arrow to travel accurately to its mark."

Your face, hands, and shiny bow-and-arrow parts are details deer don't overlook, so you shouldn't either.

If a ground blind is made of natural materials, be sure it matches surrounding features. Claude once hunted with a guy who couldn't figure why he hadn't seen any deer from his ground blind while everyone else in the hunting group was not only seeing deer but getting shots at game. Finally, Claude accompanied him to his hunting spot and quickly saw the problem. It was late fall and all the leaves had dropped from trees. So the prominent cover was bare branches and lifeless looking sticks. The guy had made his blind near two well-used deer trails, but he'd used dark green fir and cedar boughs—as out of place on the barren Michigan oak ridge as a hound at a cat show.

Complete head-to-toe camouflage clothing is even more important for low-level bowhunters than it is for tree-stand archers. Faces, hands, and shiny bow-and-arrow parts are details deer don't overlook, so you shouldn't either. And gloves and masks not only offer concealment, but also protect hunters from mosquitoes and other insects, allowing them to sit longer, with less movement—and eliminating any need for odorous bug repellents that deer can detect from long range.

There are dozens of great camo patterns on the market; just match the hues to your hunting area. If you're in dark, leafy cover, wear dark, leafy camo. If your blind is pine and cedar, mimic it with your camo clothing. Same for cactus and sage, bare branches, autumn leaves, even snow. Blend in with the blind and "break" your human silhouette.

Even with perfect camo, move a bow for a shot only when an animal is looking away, has its head down to feed, or is in cover, its view of you blocked. Should a deer look directly at you, freeze. Some bowhunters never look directly into the eyes of a deer that's looking at them. When they're being "eyeballed" by a nearby deer, they shut their eyes, believing the animal can see the unnatural glassy reflection of their human eyes.

Sometimes a "Mexican stand-off" with whitetails can last many long minutes, and holding a bow at the "ready" position can be very tiring. Resting a bow's lower limb wheel on the ground can save the day while you wait for a good shooting opportunity. Be sure to clear the inside of a blind of noisy leaves and twigs; resting a lower bow limb wheel quietly on a soft ground cloth or carpet remnant also makes sense.

"Do not sit flat on the ground in a blind," insists Claude. "Sitting on a stump, log, or big rock is better, because it's easier to raise and draw a bow with very little movement. When sitting flat on the ground, an archer must rise to his knees to raise a bow high enough to shoot. This much movement not only is quickly spotted by deer, but the more movement, the more likely the chance for noise. Sitting on a plastic bucket turned upside-down is good, as this affords plenty of lower bow-limb clearance when a shot is made. A dove stool is a perfect ground-blind seat, and I like camouflage lightweight folding aluminum-cloth ones that have a carrying strap. Folding camp stools also work well. They're easily packed to a hunting location, are silent to use, and plenty comfortable. Some even have large pockets for packing snacks, water, and bowhunting accessories."

Bowmen should be conscious of sounds their clothing makes inside blinds. Soft cotton and wool are great for close-quarters ground-blind hunting, while scratchy nylon and some Cordura products, rubbed against brush or limbs, are not so "quiet." Even the slightest sound at ground level alerts mature whitetails.

"The best-made, most camouflaged blind—one even thoroughly doused with deer cover scent—must be positioned correctly in relation to the wind for even a meticulously scent-free bowhunter to be consistently successful," Claude states. "A buck that's three, four or five years old has had plenty of experience with humans, and he's not about to make a mistake regarding wind direction. The wind is a whitetail's greatest ally, and he knows it. So when you're building a ground blind

"The best-made, most camouflaged blind—even one thoroughly doused with deer cover scent—must be positioned correctly in relation to the wind for even a meticulously scent-free bowhunter to be consistently successful," states Claude.

near a trail, creek crossing, scrape or rub line, take careful note of the wind.

"As a general rule, the best place to build a ground blind is crosswind, and slightly downwind, of the place you expect to see deer. If you build a blind directly downwind, a deer will nail you with his nose as he moves toward the place you plan to make your shot. The better position is crosswind from the direction you anticipate deer moving into the area. Even then, be clean, wear full camo, use cover scents, and don't move a muscle until time to shoot."

As always, in an area where wind direction is variable, it's often smart to build more than one blind, then hunt the best spot according to wind direction. Over the last few years, some excellent commercially made portable ground blinds have been developed. They are lightweight, extremely portable, and set up in seconds, which allows a bowman to place a blind wherever it's advantageous on a particular day. Such blinds also save hunters the time and effort of gathering brush, limbs, logs, etc.

One type of commercial blind that works well is simply a length of camo material, with a few stakes that hold it up just high enough to conceal a bowhunter sitting on a stool. It's rather short, with no roof; the camo material, about 16-feet long, attaches to five small poles which can be easily pushed into the ground. This blind can be set up in less than two minutes, rolls tightly into a shoulder-pack, and is extremely lightweight—and that portability is why it's used by many turkey hunters. Also, it's available in five camo patterns and a realistic leaf-type cloth that, from 10 feet, looks like the real thing.

Portable blinds resembling mini-tents have become well entrenched with deer bowhunters. Most have roofs or tops of some kind, four to six sides, and the best models set up and break down fast, and fold easily into compact carrying cases. Many such blinds have no floor, but the good ones are comfortably large and have zip-out windows for easy shooting. You remove the blind from its carrying case, give it a good shake, and in seconds you have a camo tent-blind within bow range of a trail, scrape or other hunting spot, preferably nestled into natural foliage. Just unzip a window or two for shooting on the side game is expected.

It's tempting to sit in such a blind near open windows, watching for game and believing arrow clearance is optimum. But Claude advises sitting on a dove stool or bucket well back from open windows, in the shadows so that bow movement is less visible to deer, and there's less chance of any blind interference when you're drawing a bow or loosing an arrow.

Ground blinds may never replace tree stands for bowhunting whitetail deer. But there are times and places where an archer who stays on terra firma will have a better chance at tagging a buster buck than the one who spends his time searching for suitable trees to "hang in."

"Let deer sign tell you where to set your ambush, not the availability of tree stand sites," says Claude. >

Claude Pollington owns Buck Pole Archery Shop in Marion, Michigan, as well as the C.P. Oneida Bow Company. He is a lifelong bowhunter who started with a long bow and cedar arrows, and has over 500 whitetails to his credit, including archery bucks sporting up to 180-inches of rack.

PHOTO BY DAVID RICHEY

A Trophy Hunter's Mind

WITH BOB ROBB

"You've got to 'get your mind right'
to hunt big bucks."

B ob Robb started his deer season in hot fashion, arrowing a heavy-beam eight-pointer that scored over 140 inches. It looked like a banner year for "big boys" for the widely traveled whitetail hunter from Alaska, who set his standards high, and kept his travel plans on track. He was determined not to collect another buck less than the 140-incher that season, and he kept his word—passing no less than six other bucks similar to the 140-incher in size while hunting in several states.

"I knew if I held out and waited for a really great buck, I'd get my chance at a true monster," Bob says lightheartedly. "But it just wasn't to be. I saw some great bucks, and got close to collecting one on several occasions. But I never shot another good buck that year because I wouldn't settle for anything less than a trophy whitetail over 140 inches.

You've got to settle for nothing less than your big-deer goal, and it's of paramount importance you have complete dedication to that bowhunting ambition, Bob Robb states emphatically.
CREDIT BOB ROBB.

"Seems sort of crazy, now that I think about it and talk about it. But that's what a trophy-seeking whitetail bowhunter has got to decide for himself. He has to determine what he's going to be satisfied harvesting. Then he's got to have the self discipline to stick with that decision—no matter what the end result."

Although Bob failed to collect a buck better than his first 140-incher that year, he has no regrets "passing" those other bucks. He'd gotten "his mind right" long before he saw those deer, and knew they wouldn't qualify as trophies for his season. Tightly focused on a better buck, he stuck to the course he'd planned. Although he went home without much venison or racks for his den wall, it was okay; he could live with it. Because a hunter looking for a trophy must be willing to accept failure and just keep going, learning and looking for better deer in better places.

It's sometimes hard to do, but that "trophy-buck mindset" is something anyone can develop with some conscious effort, says Bob.

"A lot of 'in-the-trenches' legwork is involved in trophy buck hunting, most of it careful research carried out long before season begins," explains Bob. "But it's good training in how to get 'your mind right' and focused on very specific, high-quality animals."

The first thoughtful step to tagging trophy deer is learning where you are most likely to find them, advises Bob. This doesn't necessarily mean targeting only the notable big-buck states, like Kansas, Kentucky, Iowa, Illinois, and Ohio. The same "digging" for choice trophy buck spots can be done anywhere, even in your own backyard, if that's the only place where you can bowhunt.

"Since all deer country, even in a comparatively small region, is not equally productive, it's imperative for 'trophy' chasers to do a lot of study to determine where they should spend the bulk of their hunting hours," explains Bob. "Too many bowmen automatically assume that the biggest, most popular, and well-known states and hunting zones offer the best chances for collecting trophy deer. But such an assumption may be false.

"Many places well known for big deer have a tremendous amount of hunting pressure—especially commercial, guided operations—and so are not as good for trophy deer as harvest reports might lead one to believe. For example, I know an Illinois county that is world renowned for giving up huge numbers of record-book bucks. The area still produces about the same number of big deer as it did 15 years ago, but today 10 times the number of bowhunters work it. So the odds of a bowhunter collecting a true trophy from that county are considerably less than they were a decade ago.

"Interestingly, a lesser-known county in an adjoining state, only a three-hour drive from the famous one in Illinois, is a much better spot to tag a heavy-beam buck. It receives comparatively little intelligent bowhunting pressure, and the ratio of hunting man-hours per trophy deer tagged is much better."

Bob says the lesser-known area is overlooked by legions of bowmen who rush headlong to Illinois, believing the renowned spot is the only place worth bowhunting for giant whitetails. But they are wrong.

There are many ways to learn a locale's best spots for big deer, according to Bob. Some are easy to follow, others are not, but they all require a purposeful, careful mindset to fulfill your goal of taking a trophy deer.

Among the best sources of information are wildlife department personnel. Start at the state level with the chief of deer management and ask him to recommend what he considers the best big-deer counties in his state. Learn if there are any special management projects under way to grow trophy-class deer via strict limits, minimum rack requirements, or quality deer management (QDM) techniques.

Sometimes, small overlooked hunting areas are targeted by such programs (even "experimental" ones) and can offer outstanding opportunities for taking huge deer. Other times military installations, federal refuges or even state parks are open to bowhunting on a limited or lottery basis. Not all of these hunts are well publicized, and unless you "dig" and ask about them, you'll never know they're taking place.

Ask about new wildlife-management areas that may be opening. Often a new state-run spot only has been lightly (or never) hunted for several years, which frequently results in the age class of mature bucks increasing dramatically. And the more older deer there are around, the better your odds for tagging a trophy.

"After you have the names of a few good deer counties in a chosen deer state, learn who the regional wildlife biologist is in charge of them," Bob advises. "A tremendous amount of information can be garnered from game biologists and managers, since they're in the field all the time, doing research, watching animals, making deer counts and helping with wildlife plantings, etc. Ask about any trophy bucks recently taken in his area: Who took them, when and where. Don't be shy. Most game managers are pleasant and very helpful to bowhunters, including non-residents, since their primary job is basically to help people with hunting."

Bob says in many areas, big-deer contests are held. If the top buck consistently comes from one region or county, it's a good bet the area has a better-than-average population of trophy game. Local newspaper outdoor writers can also put hunters onto potential big-deer spots. Most of them keep abreast of "hot" deer zones, and many know of "sleeper" spots, too. You also may learn about them through commercial hunting operations, sporting-goods shops, hunting-camp owners, and guides.

Sometimes the very best big-deer spots are so small, underrated or overlooked, virtually no one hunts them, Bob Robb contends.

"Be friendly in your questioning of these people, and try to 'soft-sell' your purpose of seeking big deer information," Bob declares. "These folks easily can be turned off by a pushy out-of-stater only interested in his quest for giant deer. But polite inquiries about a region's whitetails, where larger bucks are downed, when, and how, can provide a wealth of trophy-deer knowledge.

"If you decide a commercial deer lodge or guided operation is the way to go, be sure to talk to several good ones who know the area you want to tap for big deer. Outdoor writers, game department personnel, satisfied clients or knowledgeable friends who have nothing to personally gain, can often recommend guides.

"When speaking with guides, tell them you're only interested in big deer—a personal trophy. Explain you want the buck for mounting, a wall buster or nothing. Be up front about your intentions and expectations, and it's likely you'll learn a great deal about the state, area and guide or deer camp you've targeted for visiting. Ask about prime times for big deer, how guides work for trophies, what's expected of you, and how much 'latitude' is allowed for your bow-hunting."

Bowhunters should be sure to learn from guides if they allow clients to scout; if bowmen can stillhunt; whether it's all-day hunting or only mornings and afternoons? Guides who take time to provide such information likely are good ones who truly know about big deer in the region you intend to hunt, Bob says.

"Sometimes the very best big-deer spots are so small, underrated or overlooked that virtually no one hunts them," Bob contends. "Even state biologists have no inkling what the little spots contain. I call these places 'do-it-yourself areas,' because there's no other way to learn about them except by exploring and testing them yourself. Contrary to most trophy-deer beliefs, there are plenty of public hunting lands like this.

"In many places, like Wisconsin for example, there are county-owned lands and WMAs that are so small (only a few hundred acres), most deer hunters ignore them or don't know about them. In other states, like Illinois and Missouri, there are places like 'waterfowl-management areas' that are open only to bow deer hunting, and they are incredible big buck havens. They're sometimes tough to hunt, and it takes a lot of legwork to learn about these spots. But it's part of the thoughtful process of targeting trophy bucks other people bypass."

Extensive development around a hunting area turns off a lot of trophy-deer chasers, but it can be deceiving in determining a spot's potential, Bob reports. One of the best Michigan deer havens he ever heard about was a series of woods strips along creeks near posh homes. The place bordered a private country club and all the residents were golfers and tennis buffs. No one bothered the abundant and oversize deer. So getting permission to bowhunt the area from homeowners, who couldn't grow flowers and often had vehicle collisions with whitetails, was easy.

Bob had a friend on a South Carolina country club coastal island who got permission to bowhunt club property, but only on Mondays when the place was closed to golfers. Every Monday, Bob's buddy had the club to himself, and he collected a lot of deer, including several dandy bucks.

Bob emphasizes that once you've targeted several good trophy-buck spots you know hold healthy whitetails, stick with them. Don't spread yourself too thin bowhunting too many different and far-flung places. Spend time learning everything there is to know about those very few, well-chosen, trophy-deer locations. Get to know where the choicest deer-bedding areas are located; where doe and fawn groups are concentrated; where rutting ridges and food sources are found. Only by thoroughly learning such things about a deer spot, and by hunting it constantly, can you have complete confidence that the trophy whitetails you know exist there will eventually succumb to your hunting skills.

"Timing also is an important part of a trophy-buck mindset," Bob insists. "Simply stated, a bowman should be on the prowl when the 'time is right' for tagging heavyweight whitetails. This means avoiding hot and dry weather conditions and being afield at peak times—such as daybreak, dusk and during the rut. These 'prime times' also can vary dramatically in different locations, and if you've done your homework, you can hopscotch from one great spot to the next, being there during ideal times to collect trophies.

This kind of deer bowhunting isn't for everyone, and certainly not all the time. But if you commit to it, hold solid to the mindset that you will only down a massive-rack buck or shoot no whitetail at all.

"Last year, for example, a friend and I started in Illinois, getting there just as the rut started. We scored well and moved into Kentucky, where we hit the rut just right, too. From there we moved on to Iowa, where we lucked out again. It was a two-week hunt, and I had to head home, while my pal moved on to Kansas, where he was lucky enough to draw a tag. His first day hunting, he collected a 175-inch buck."

Trophy-buck mindset and perfect timing are two essential keys to giant whitetail success, Bob maintains.

Finally, it's important that all sportsmen who seek whopper whitetails assume a "big-buck attitude."

"You've got to settle for nothing less than your big-deer goal, and it's of paramount importance you have complete dedication to that bowhunting ambition," Bob states emphatically. "You must have total confidence in your bowhunting skills, and be firmly committed to your efforts. This kind of deer bowhunting isn't for everyone, and certainly not all the time. But if you commit to it, hold solid to the mindset that you will only down a massive-rack buck or shoot no whitetail at all. This is exactly what a bowhunter's mental attitude should be regarding trophy bucks. Settle for nothing less than your big deer goal, and it's likely you'll eventually attain the prize of your dreams." >

Bob Robb, who recently moved from Alaska to Arizona, is editor of Whitetail Journal *magazine. He has hunted from western Canada to the Carolina coast, from the upper Midwest to the Deep South, and has arrowed hundreds of whitetails, including over 30 that would qualify for the Pope & Young record book. His best buck is an Illinois 10-pointer gross-scoring 180⅜ inches.* CREDIT BOB ROBB.

Draw a Doe, Bust a Buck

WITH TERRY HEAD

"Find does in quantity, and when the time is right, bucks will come looking for you."

It was a late afternoon well before the rut, early October, in fact, and Terry Head of Oklahoma City was high in a bow tree stand overlooking a steep draw to a tangled bottom. As the sun slowly settled into the timber tops, long shadows crept over the understory, and the air temperature dropped noticeably. Wildlife was on the move. Gray squirrels did their Tarzan routine. A fox foraged a hillside. A barred owl cut loose with a long, loud series of hoots and screeches.

Prime time to be bowhunting. So Terry stood in his stand, arrow already nocked, watching a trail crossing just 18 yards upwind.

He heard the deer long before he saw it, and figured it was a yearling, probably the button buck who'd become his little buddy. Bold and frisky, the bristle-face nubbin buck bounded from the bottom thicket where Terry knew he bedded. The young deer dashed up the hillside, stopping just 10 steps from Terry's stand, and began feeding on the bright-green white oak acorns that crowded the ground. Three huge oaks within bow range of his tree stand were raining acorns, and tracks and droppings under them left no doubt it was a high deer-traffic area.

A few minutes passed, and another yearling tracked the little buck, soon followed by a large, gray-faced doe. Terry had seen the same three deer from the stand every time he'd hunted it over the past two weeks. The doe was a tempting target, especially early in the season. But Terry's personal rule is never to arrow a doe with young. Does needed to be cropped off the property he hunted. But that's something best done after the rut, thought Terry, when fawns are on their own, and bucks aren't so likely to be sniffing the periphery of a potential harem.

Find the does (background, left), and you'll locate bucks, says Terry Head.

So Terry waited and watched. Over the next 30 minutes, the white oak acorn restaurant at his feet became a wide-open free-for-all buffet. Nine deer were soon feeding around the oaks, all does with yearlings. There were so many deer that it was difficult for Terry to move on his stand without a white-tail picking him off. He was frozen, at least until he spotted a big buck easing up from the draw, well wide of the does, but very interested in their buffet.

He was a decent eight-pointer, high rack, good mass, but no more than a two-and-a-half-year old. While Terry considered whether he'd try a shot if he worked closer to the tree stand, Terry suddenly noticed a much bigger buck trailing the eight-pointer up the ridge. Both were focused hard on the feeding does, and while not in the least bit spooked, they acted, well, like bucks—cagey, careful, noses frequently held high to test the wind, and watchful of the bevy of beauties.

The bigger buck was a heavy, mature 10-pointer, maybe Pope & Young material. Terry switched on his mental green light for shooting, and the buck became his focused guest of honor.

The bucks walked a faint trail paralleling the does, and slowly angled Terry's way, toward the white oak acorn buffet. Terry figured they'd work within 25 yards, offering a good broadside shot, and he prepared for it slowly—careful to move only when the does beneath him were head down, and none of the deer alert.

At 30 yards, the bucks moved ever so cautiously wide of the does, feeding and watching. As the big 10-pointer glided into an opening, Terry raised his bow, drew, and anchored comfortably—sight pin settling quickly behind the buck's shoulder. He almost touched off the shot, but didn't like the angle. The buck was moving to a better, more open position, and the bowman waited at full draw.

But when the 10-pointer got there, a vine covered his rib cage, then the deer slipped behind a tree. Terry had to let down his compound, and the small opportunity window for shooting disappeared as the bucks turned slightly and fed up the ridge, away from the does.

Terry was disappointed, but held in his frustration, careful not to spook his does. It paid off, because two weeks later, as the rut began to tickle bucks in all the right places, Terry's son, T.J., shot a magnificent 140-inch buck from the same stand. T.J. saw three bucks that morning—all with does, or following them.

This underscores the patience and persistence needed to be consistently successful in buck hunting, explains Terry Head; patience to wait for the right buck and the right moment for shooting. Persistence is vital in finding does and being careful not to spook them, so that when their suitors come calling during the rut, you can sight on a racked target of your choice.

Using does to attract bucks is nothing new to knowledgeable, successful bowhunters. But there are plenty of archers who still shoot every doe they have an opportunity to arrow, then wonder why they're not seeing and killing bucks.

"There's nothing wrong with shooting does with bows," says Terry. "In fact, I still get a great kick out of making a good, clean shot on a doe with a well-placed arrow. But these days, rarely do I shoot a doe until long after the rut is over. That can get pretty challenging, because does are more spooky by then, and foliage is off trees, so deer can more easily pick you off a tree stand.

"I don't shoot many does early in the season, not only because most have fawns in tow, but because I don't want does in my hunt areas spooky or afraid to come close to my ambush sites. I want them relaxed, contented as fat cows in a pasture, as unafraid of humans as deer in a petting zoo. In fact, in the very best places I have for bowhunting—stands that are smack in the middle of mast-heavy white oaks, or around fields of CRP, corn or soybeans—I stay

Does draw bucks, which is why Terry prefers doe decoys.

out of the area until the rut starts. I check those spots a time or two in preparing stands, and verify if the mast crop looks good and trails are active from doe and yearling traffic. But I don't bowhunt those hot doe spots until bucks are on the move, at least in the pre-rut.

"If I shot the first doe I had a chance to thump from such a spot, not only would it alert other deer to my presence, but in tracking a doe and hauling her out of the woods, I'm contaminating an area with human activity and scent. That might not bother a few yearlings in an area, or even a young buck or two. But for mature bucks (and old does), you can't get away with such intrusion into their core home range without alerting them, putting them on defense, and likely disrupting their usual routines."

Terry believes a deer doesn't have to live and feed right where you've seen his sign, or actually seen him repeatedly. Push him or spook him a bit, and he can just as easily live a half-mile away on another tract of land where no one bothers him. Or he can become nocturnal—a deer devil in the darkness—and, perhaps, impossible to kill.

"Early in bow season, if I want a doe, I'll bowhunt public property, a place I know will be overrun with hunters when the general firearms season starts about the time the rut kicks in," Terry says. "Such places get so much pressure during gun season that odds of me arrowing a good buck on the property then are almost nil.

"But in the early bow-only season, hunters are scarce, does are available and unmolested. If I zip one, I'm unconcerned about disturbing other deer, including bucks. Because when the rut starts and guns boom, I head to my private hunt property, where we only hunt with bows, deer are calm, relaxed, and I know when and where they're feeding."

By then, Terry has pinpointed doe concentrations and has stand sites on trails to intercept bucks as they roam among single females looking for love.

Locating doe hang-outs isn't difficult, Terry contends. Find choice deer food, and does and yearlings should be there in quantity. In farm country, he uses binoculars to check doe spots, like woodlot corners tucked back in secluded corn, wheat, soybean and alfalfa fields. When he finds a doe family unit or two, he patterns them to see if they habitually use a specific field spot, noting the time they show up.

He learns when they cross an old logging road, or enter an abandoned apple orchard, or feed under a stand of persimmon or honey locust trees. But he stays out of the area until the rut starts to rock—at least, if he wants a good buck. Then Terry waits for the right wind and weather conditions before making his move.

"One indicator that conditions are getting right to hunt a doe spot for mature bucks is when you start seeing yearling, nubbin bucks alone," explains Terry. "They're single because does have run them off in preparation for being receptive to dominant bucks. The rut is then approaching and it's time to get serious about moving into doe bedrooms you've discovered or cultivated."

Setting a stand mid-day in such a place is a good idea, according to Terry. And it's been his experience that the first time or two he hunts the spot are the best chances he'll get at a mature buck as he checks "his" does. Be careful not to over-hunt a spot, he cautions. And be mindful not to bust does, or you'll run off bucks, too.

In states where hunting over game feeders or bait piles is legal, hunters often say that such places aren't choice for downing a buster buck. Don't believe it, says Terry. Plant a clover field. Hang a game feeder with corn. In a secluded woods, dump a pile of sugar beats, carrots, apples or acorns raked from your backyard. When does show up, sooner or later bucks will, too, he reports. Just be sure to treat does with care, nurturing them to be safe, calm and happy.

"Does are your buck bait," he says smiling. "Time your bowhunt right and you should see every big rack in the area sniffing around your does. Sort of like frat boys at a sorority dance.

"But don't forget that you've still got to bowhunt bucks like they're the sharp-senses animals they are. Locate does, stay out of the area until bucks get rut frisky. Then set stands in choice areas to ambush your racked quarry as they approach the places does reside. Use cover and camouflage to your best advantage. Check wind direction. Climb high in stands. And be sure your bow is quiet, and your shooting form is well honed.

"Arrowing a Pope & Young-class buck is never easy. But bowhunting around doe bait is a step in the right direction."

Decoy Tactics

Bowmen who have done their homework, and learned where there are concentrations of does, have located hot spots for using decoys to lure mature bucks within arrow range. But there's a lot more to using fake whitetails than simply placing them around a tree stand and expecting every buck in the area to come prancing in. Decoys can be an archer's ace-in-the-hole for arrowing a buck with a good rack—provided they're well made and correctly used.

Many bowmen prefer full-body 3-D-size models: large, sturdy, and able to stand up to strong wind and other rigors of hunting. They have removable legs, a head, and ears that fit inside hollow decoy "shells," which makes them portable. But such decoys still can be a bear to tote more than a few hundred yards if you're also carrying a tree stand, bow, and a pack. Thank goodness for ATVs.

Although lugging around decoys can be a chore, it's one that's well worthwhile. Over the years, Terry Head has downed a number of heavy-beam bucks using full-size doe decoys, and he's adamant that decoys lure bucks into range, especially during the rut. His decoys also have attachable small plastic antlers, which can be used to simulate a small buck—the idea being that it enrages and draws in bigger, more dominant bucks. But Terry says he's done much better with doe decoys.

"I try not to touch a decoy with bare hands, only with rubber gloves," he says. "I usually transport a decoy in a bright-orange mesh bag for safety, and take it close to a hunt area on an ATV or truck. This way, human scent is kept to a minimum on the decoy."

He also says that using a couple of decoys can be very effective, and handling them is easy if you're using a vehicle to carry them in.

Terry prefers to wear rubber gloves when moving around and touching decoys.

At times Terry pours doe estrus scent on his fake deer, which not only attracts bucks, but helps mask any foreign odor that may have settled on the dekes, although the hard plastic shell is non-absorbent. "Smoke" scents, such as those made by Deer Quest can be good because a bowman need not handle a decoy, or even be very close to it, to properly utilize the smoke's aromas to attract whitetails.

Terry doesn't transport decoys to and from his stand site daily, but rather leaves them in his hunt area. However, when he's not on stand, he removes decoys from the chosen site and, placing them on their sides, hides them in bushes or grass. This way, deer moving through an area don't suspect decoys are fake, and then ignore them when Terry is hunting the spot.

Positioning decoys correctly is important to successfully arrowing a good buck. Terry usually sets decoys upwind, facing away from his stand, because a buck invariably approaches doe decoys from the rear

Terry says what really makes a decoy bring bucks in close is tail movement. Not all decoys come with a tail, so Terry installs a real doe tail, bolting it to a decoy at its stern. He positions a fake doe in a woods opening, fire break, or field edge so any approaching buck sees the tail from long range. To the tail, Terry ties heavy-duty, abrasion-resistant braided fishing line from a push-button fishing reel.

"I take the reel up to my tree stand," he explains. "When I see a buck look-ing at the decoy, all I've got to do is pull on the fishing reel, and that makes the doe tail wave or swish back and forth. It's incredible how well it works, espe-cially when a decoy is on a field edge. Any rutting buck that's alone and sees my doe gets interested. When her tail wiggles, he's on the way over to check her out right now! I've drawn huge bucks from several hundred yards by swishing a decoy tail.

"Sometimes, making just a few grunts on a call so enrages a reluctant buck, that he actually runs to my decoy. I think a buck hears that grunt, sees a doe tail wiggling, and figures another buck he can't see is tending the doe—and that makes him go crazy. It's a great tactic for bowmen looking for a heavy-antler buck." >

Terry Head is a native of Oklahoma, with many years of bowhunting experience in deer-rich Missouri. He has taken numerous whitetails and a number of buster bucks.

Never Stop Grunting

WITH WILL PRIMOS

"Grunt calling reverses the hunting tables. Instead of you looking for a buck, the buck comes looking for you."

I t was a week before his biggest whitetail deer hunt of the season, a six-day trip to middle Georgia, in a county where, the previous year, a pair of Boone & Crockett bucks had been tagged. Like every serious deer hunter, this prominent bowman was ready long before the eve of the trip. All gear was packed and set to go. Tree stands had been in place for weeks. The sportsman knew the hunt property like his backyard, and every time he watched television weather, he longed and prayed for cool nights and approaching cold fronts to kick bucks into activity.

Everything was going perfectly as he counted the days until departure. Then he got a package in the mail that drastically changed his hunt and, in fact, altered his deer bowhunting from that day until now.

It was a plain brown envelope, and when he opened it, there were a pair of hard plastic tubes, obviously calls of some type. But they looked different than a standard goose or duck call. When he blew into one, the call made a sound sort of like a bull on steroids. A letter in the envelope from Will Primos said that the tubes were new, designed to "call" deer, and they worked—if they were used correctly.

The bowman had known Will for years and had hunted with him often. If Will said the call worked, he had to give Will the benefit of the doubt. With his big deer hunt approaching, the archer phoned Will to get the inside scoop on his new deer call.

"I'm tellin' ya, it works; we're really on to something here," Will told the bowhunter on the phone. "This is the hottest thing in deer hunting, and it's going to be huge when the word gets out about how effective this calling technique is.

"I've been working with deer for months, listening to them, designing and perfecting a call that sounds just like they do. I've worked out some of the calls bucks make, and I've tried it in the wild and have been pretty darned successful."

The hunter asked Will why a deer calls, and why in 30 years hunting whitetails in two dozen states, he had never heard a deer make a call.

While not every deer responds to calling, rarely are they spooked by it.

Will said that deer call all the time, and had a pretty extensive "vocabulary." But their calls are soft, subtle sounds, which is why most sportsmen never hear them.

"I'm sure you've heard deer call, you just didn't know what the sounds were," Will continued. "Once I spent time near a deer pen, I started to realize all the different sounds deer make. My ears got kind of 'tuned' to their noises, too, and that's when I started to pick up on those sounds in the woods. The idea of deer calling to one another really isn't too radical when you think about all the other wildlife that call. Birds do it all the time. So do elk, raccoons, otters, coyotes, wolves, frogs, crickets, lots of critters.

"We all know how smart deer are. So it makes sense they have evolved to the point they can communicate via sound."

It all made sense, especially coming from Will, thought the hunter. In fact, sitting there talking to Will on the phone, he started getting fidgety thinking about his upcoming Georgia hunt. The archer told Will about it, and asked for a crash course in deer calling.

"The most important thing is to believe in the deer call," Will explained. "Heck, it's not going to work every time on every deer. No call does that. You can call to a dozen flocks of ducks or geese or 10 different gobblers before you get one to respond the way you want. The same occurs with deer. Not every buck comes running to your call. But it will work, and it will bring in deer, if you stay with grunting and do it the right way.

"I keep my call on a lanyard around my neck, tucked inside my shirt or jacket. Every 15 or 20 minutes—by the watch—I take out the call and lightly blow into it, calling aggressively for 15 to 30 seconds. Most people call much too loud and way too often. Deer calls are subtle and soft, and it's important only to call for a few seconds at a time. A deer can hear even soft calls for hundreds of yards. It's unnatural to call too long or too loud. Done right, you'll never spook a deer with a grunt call. It can only help you, never hurt your hunting."

Will's words were radical back then, many years ago. But he was so enthusiastic, so captivated by deer calling, that the long-experienced bowman believed Will and asked for a phone demonstration.

Will called with his grunt tube into the phone, and the hunter listened intently to the soft, hog-like sounds. They were broken notes of long and short duration, and he made the sounds for only 30 seconds.

"After you do that, put your call away and be patient," Will continued. "In 20 minutes, grunt again for 20 or 30 seconds. Just do it softly and not too often. Stay with it during your Georgia hunt, and I bet you'll be amazed what happens."

The hunter grunted with his new call into the phone. Will listened carefully and in just a few minutes fine-tuned the bowman's skills until he had a reasonable buck sound coming from his end of the line. The archer thanked Will, hung up, and continued practicing over the next several days—including outside in an "open" environment, at Will's suggestion.

He had the grunt call in his pack that first dawn on stand in Georgia. It was cool enough to wear a lined jacket, and there was no wind. The woods were so still, he could hear woodpeckers hammering from hundreds of yards away. Barred owls hooted loud enough to terrorize turkeys for miles. It was a day designed for deer hunting.

Conditions were so perfect, so, well, "bucky," that the hunter couldn't get himself to use the grunt call. He was afraid of spooking nearby deer he didn't see. Grunting—making noise of any kind—was completely, totally, 180-degrees against the grain of everything he'd been taught and trained to do in over a generation of deer hunting. So those first few hours on stand, the archer simply sat there watching and waiting for a chance at a buck. By 10 a.m., he had seen or heard nothing but squirrels and birds.

Finally, slight movement 50 yards away caught his eye. As minutes passed, he saw a large doe feeding across an oak ridge. He watched her for 20 minutes and saw no other deer, and she acted as though she were alone. She was the perfect first audience for his new grunt call, so he slowly pulled it from his pack, brought it to his lips, and in his best Will Primos tone, blew softly into it.

Her reaction was startling—at least to him. She completely ignored it. Didn't so much as twitch an ear or wiggle her nose. So he grunted again, this time louder. Her head was down, feeding, and when

Bowmen who stick with grunt calling will enjoy success, according to Will.

the archer called she froze, but didn't raise her head. The bowman knew she heard the grunt, but again she completely ignored it, and continued feeding, wandering slowly out of sight.

Score one for the grunt call, thought the bowman. At least it didn't spook deer.

Over the next hour, he grunted just like Will instructed, without seeing another deer. But late that afternoon, things changed.

He sat in the same stand at 3 p.m., and every 20 minutes, grunted softly with his call. Nothing happened over the course of the next two hours. Though conditions were perfect, he'd seen no deer. Then, finally, he grunted at 5 p.m., and instantly a heavy-body eight-point buck bounced up and out of a nearby ravine only 30 yards away. The buck must have been walking along in it, but the hunter hadn't known he was there until he blew the call, and the buck bounded stiff-legged up the ridge where the tree stand was hanging on an oak.

The deer never grunted back; he never made a sound. But he was obviously looking for the source of the call. The hairs on his back were raised, and he was on full alert. The shot was an easy one, and the bowman collected his first good buck with a grunt call.

The hunter has downed dozens of whitetails since then, and he's convinced many were attracted into shooting range by a grunt call. Like Will said, it doesn't work every day in the deer woods. But grunt calls can be so effective—at virtually any time during deer season—that they are an integral part of many veteran whitetail hunters' woods routine—an essential, "always-go" item in deer-hunting daypacks nationwide.

Over the last 20 years or so, scientists and many hunters have learned that whitetails are very vocal animals, and definitely do communicate. Wildlife biologists Dr. Larry Marchinton and Dr. Tom Atkeson of the University of Georgia's School of Forest Resources have determined that whitetail deer have at least 12 different vocalizations. Larry Richardson of Mississippi State University, who has also studied deer calling, agrees that whitetail grunting is a complicated form of deer's social communication.

"To understand how a grunt deer call works, it's important to realize it is like any other animal call," explains Will Primos. "Calling deer is much like calling turkeys. When you see a buck coming to you, don't call. If the buck stops and turns away before he's within shooting distance, give a light, soft call. Only when the buck turns away and is no longer facing in your direction should you give another call.

"Location calling is important, too. Choosing just the right spot to call deer from is very important to success and something not enough bow-hunters consider. It's not only important to call and get a deer's attention, but you have to be in a spot where deer can't readily see you. You want

137

Will says most deer hunters have heard bucks grunting, but usually don't recognize the subtle, soft calls that deer make.

a deer that's heard your call to come looking for you. A good place for calling might be the back of a cane thicket, or some other place where a buck has got to expose himself—in bow range—to find the source of the call."

Will believes many hunters are confused about what's best, a deep, throaty grunt or a high, shrill one. Actually, both are effective, he says.

"Some people think big bucks grunt low and gravely, while small bucks squeak," he explains. "But deer have different voice tones, and they grunt for many different reasons. I've seen spikes with low, base grunt tones, and eight-pointers with squeaky grunts.

"In my experience, the grunt call is best used in areas where deer are allowed to act like deer. The call is not as effective in places where deer are constantly harassed by dogs or hunters. It's also most deadly on 1½- to 2½-year-old bucks. It works very well on does, because the animals are gregarious and always seeking others of their kind.

"I'm convinced that when a hunter uses a call correctly, it's impossible for him to alarm or scare deer. I've watched too many deer react to a call positively for it to alarm them. I've also called to lots of deer I had no intention of shooting. The animals either come to the call, or ignore it. They never spook."

A basic calling sequence requires 15 to 20 short "hoggy" grunts, one behind the other over about 30 seconds, like a person hyperventilating, contends Will. Then put the call aside and watch for deer. A deer can easily hear even a low call out to about 300 yards—their ears are "tuned" to it— especially on a calm, clear, cold morning. They'll usually come to a call slowly, kind of sneaking in, so you've got to be alert and ready for a shot. Deer come in looking for you—much like a turkey will—because they're looking for a deer that made the sound. Often, it takes a deer coming to a call 15 to 20 minutes to work its way close enough to an archer for a shot.

It's a good idea to cup your hand over the end of a grunt call, much like a duck or crow call, states Will. Blow the call low and against your chest. Another good tactic is to move the call slowly from left to right, or vice versa, when grunting. This not only simulates a moving buck, but helps increase the range of a call by sending out sounds in different directions. Always remember that it's better to call too soft rather than too loud. Also, call no more than every 15 to 20 minutes, and use a watch to keep times accurate.

One exception to these basic rules, however, is when hunting in high wind or near some other sound-making source, like a river or near a busy highway, says Will. When you see a buck 200 yards away, you've got to blow a grunt call loud enough to get his attention—especially if the wind is blowing. Call more frequently to draw far-off bucks that may soon move out of hearing range.

"Deer calling will not make a great hunter out of a poor one," contends Will. "A hunter still must work to put himself in good whitetail habitat, and not be seen, heard or scented by deer before a shot is made. Also, you've got to put in the proper amount of 'grunt time' to prove its effectiveness, and become confident in its use. It's important to keep calling, keep learning about calls, and perfect your techniques. But unlike other phases of the sport, calling deer makes them come looking for you, rather than the other way around. This alone makes grunting for whitetails an interesting, fun challenge to the sport. It's the kind of tactic that allows a bowhunter to take charge and make something happen, which can keep tree-stand boredom to a minimum, and sure helps put venison in the freezer."

Doe Bleats

In recent years, doe "bleat" calls have gained wide popularity with bowhunters, and with good reason. The simple, sharp but plaintive doe bleat is an effective call for drawing whitetails within bow range from opening day of archery season until it's time to hang up bows at the end of the year.

Today, most doe bleats are made with a "can"—a simple-to-use device available from many call manufacturers. Small enough to fit easily in the palm of your hand, it only has to be turned over to emit a long-note bleat.

The call works early in the season for bringing does within bow range because they believe the bleat is from a lost fawn. Later in the year, near the rut, especially when used in conjunction with a grunt call, a bowhunter can simulate the calling made by a doe and a tending buck. Often just a simple doe bleat is enough to turn on a rutting buck and bring him running.

Later in the season, during the post-rut period, some bucks will come to a bleat call simply to learn if a late-estrus doe is available. Does also are drawn to a late bleat call, because a mother's instinct is one not easily overcome.

Rattlin' Rogues

Rattling "horns" or antlers are effective deer calls, especially in areas having high buck numbers. Rattling simulates a buck fight, presumably over a doe, which, when heard by another buck, should bring him running in hopes of stealing the distaff whitetail. When rattling is used correctly, it produces plenty of natural commotion and can be a real attraction for rut-crazed whitetails.

A good technique is to clack together a pair of antlers several times loudly, then tinkle the tines a bit to sound like a pair of rutting bucks sparring. The whole sequence should last only 30 seconds or so. Now, mix in some grunt calls, and perhaps a doe bleat. Then get ready. Use your binoculars. Scan the whole area, especially downwind and at long range.

Rattling is most effective during the

With a pair of bowmen working together, rattling can be deadly, especially if the archers are stillhunting slowly on the ground.

rut. Toting rattling antlers to and from tree stands can be troublesome, but it's worthwhile. Some "rattle bags" on the market are a good antler substitute, and most pack easily. The only downside to rattling is that bucks often come into bow range pins-and-needles alert and from downwind, which can make for a difficult archery target.

A pair of bowmen working together rattling can be deadly, especially for archers slowly stillhunting on the ground. One person rattles while the other archer waits, arrow nocked, perhaps a bit downwind from the rattling sounds. Be alert; bucks "coming to horns" often show up fast, and are quick to leave if they sense something amiss. >

Will Primos is president of Primos Game Calls and an authority on bowhunting whitetails. The Mississippi native has arrowed hundreds of deer, many huge bucks, as well as numerous other big-game animals.

Drag-Rag Bucks

WITH MATT MORRETT

"Here's one of the best ways to make a buck hunt you."

I t was Matt Morrett's first deer hunt with his dad, Tom, in the rolling hills of Pennsylvania. "I was only 12, and everything was new and exciting, but I'll never forget my dad rigging up his deer drag rag before we left our hunting vehicle at daylight on opening morning," says Matt. "He had a piece of old cloth tied to a heavy cord that was fastened to his boot. He dipped the cloth in some foul-smelling deer lure, dropped it on the ground, and we walked a long way into the woods—dragging the cloth behind us."

Matt and his dad were far off in the woods and had settled into a well-camouflaged ground blind.

"We hadn't waited very long when, sure enough, here comes a small buck with its nose to the ground following the same trail we walked on to our blind," recalls Matt. "I couldn't believe my eyes. I was just amazed. That buck absolutely tracked us to our spot, and offered me an easy shot—but I missed him.

"Dad still kids me about missing that deer. I laugh about it, too, but that lesson of using drag rags sank in, because I use them now habitually. Dad still does, of course."

Matt's father—like thousands of drag-rag advocates—made his own drag rags from old clothing or diapers cut into strips. The rags were washed in non-scent detergent, tied to lengths of heavy cord about five feet long, then stowed in plastic bags until ready for use in the deer woods. When walking to a hunting spot, a rag cord was tied to the hunter's boot or pants leg, and the rag was soaked in a favorite deer-attractant potion.

The concept of using a drag rag is pretty basic. The theory is that deer, especially bucks, are on the prowl, looking for other deer. When they cross the scent trail of a drag rag, they'll track a hunter right to his stand. It doesn't work every time, because nothing works that well. But drag rags cause the demise of plenty of bucks every autumn. Besides, according to Matt Morrett, using drag rags is easy, and sure can't hurt a hunter's success.

He says there are some important tips to follow for effective drag-rag use, however.

Before Matt climbs his tree stand, he places a drag rag on a bush nearby.

"I'm convinced that when I hear about drag rags spooking deer, it's because a hunter was careless and a buck picked up human scent somehow while tracking the drag rag," Matt contends. "It's imperative that a hunter use scent-free boots, like rubber ones, and that he spray his boots and pants legs thoroughly with odor-neutralizer before beginning a hunt.

"I'm also sure to spray all my hunting clothing with odor-neutralizer, and I wear rubber gloves. I do all this before handling a drag rag because I don't want any trace of human scent that a buck might pick up when he's tracking a rag to my stand."

Matt says it makes good sense to add deer lure to a rag a time or two as you're walking to a stand—especially if it's a long trek. This keeps a scent trail strong and helps ensure a buck that crosses a drag rag trail doesn't follow the scent the opposite way of your track. Because a deer's sense of smell is so acute, bucks can track a drag rag's scent hours after the trail was made. Many bowhunters who walked to stands dragging a rag before dawn have arrowed record-book bucks that didn't follow the trail to their stands until almost dark.

Most drag-rag advocates use doe-in-estrus scent in hope of attracting rutting bucks trolling for ladies. They believe bucks are on the move, covering lots of ground seeking does in heat. When one crosses a hot doe scent set out by a hunter's drag rag, he'll come running to within bow range.

While that drag-rag concept is solid, other scents can also be used to effectively attract deer and cover human scent any time a bowman is in the woods. Some hunters use raccoon or fox urine on their drag rags, thinking that deer, curious about raccoon and fox scent, may track a rag to its source. Sometimes drag-rag hunters use dominant buck lure scent, or food scent, like acorns or apples. Matt even uses combination scents with good results.

"One mid-November, I was bowhunting in Kansas from a ground blind," he recalls. "We were trying to shoot some video, but it was raining on the last day of our hunt, and the cameraman didn't want to get his equipment wet. But I went hunting anyway.

"I got out of the truck and, using a Hunter's Specialties 'Retract-a-Drag,' I put some doe estrus scent and dominant buck urine on the rag. I walked to the blind trailing the 'Retract-a-Drag,' then set the drag rag on a limb over a scrape near my ground blind. I was wearing plastic gloves all the time to make sure no human scent was lingering near the scrape."

Matt hadn't waited long when he spotted a heavy buck. The deer was a "shooter," and he was on a path that would cross Matt's trail to his ground blind.

"That buck crossed my trail about 60 yards from my blind," says Matt. "As soon as he hit my trail, he got a nose full of my drag-rag scent and immediately turned toward me. The rut was in full gear, and that buck was lit up from smelling my drag rag. He was frothing at the mouth, his eyes were wide, and he came right up to the scrape where my drag rag was hanging on a tree branch. I took him with my bow at seven steps—from a ground blind—and he never knew I was anywhere in his world."

The buck, a nice 11-pointer, his rack taping 143 inches, traveled about 100 yards after Matt's arrow hit him.

"I don't believe there was any way I would have taken that buck had I not used a drag rag," Matt says. "That buck would have just kept going cross country. But when he smelled my scent trail, he came to me like he was being pulled on a rope."

Despite such stories, many hunters still don't believe drag-rag tactics work consistently, nor that they are worth the messy effort of pouring scents on rags or special boot pads. But no deer-hunting tactic yet devised—calling, rattling, trailing tracks in fresh snow, stalking into the wind—works every time a sportsman enters the woods hunting for wily whitetails, says Matt. And drag rags work often enough that wise hunters should put forth the little extra effort they require.

Considering the time, labor and money that goes into all serious deer hunting, pouring a bit of scent on a rag and dragging it to your tree stand isn't much of a hassle—and the rewards can be astounding, not only during the rut, but all through bow season.

"Some hunters simply pour deer scents onto their boot soles rather than using a drag rag," says Matt. "But liquid scent on a sole rubs off and evaporates too quickly to leave much of a lasting trail, particularly if you walk several hundred yards to a stand. While it's easy to make a drag rag, there are a number of commercial scent pads on the market that do much the same thing without necessary rigging."

A fresh scrape is a choice spot for hanging a drag rag.

A number of companies market boot scent pads that pull over outer footwear. The pads, made of absorbent material, are positioned just ahead of the boot heel, against the sole, and secured with an elastic band, shoelace or some other sort of tie. Once the pad is in position on the hunter's foot, he pours the deer attractant on it. The saturated pads leave scent on the ground with each step the hunter takes—a trail deer follow easily.

Retractable drag rags, like the type Matt favors, are also good because they're easy to handle and can be placed over a scrape or bush near a stand once you arrive at a hunting site.

Making drag rags from old socks or ragged T-shirts is easy enough; a 12-inch square of cotton works well; and old, heavy, terry-cloth face towels are great, because they're very absorbent and rugged enough not to tear when dragged over rough ground, briers and rocks.

Wash the rags in non-scent soap or boil them clean, and let them dry in the sun. Never touch them without rubber gloves after they've been washed or boiled, or they'll become contaminated with human scent. Store rags in a heavy-duty, zip-seal, freezer-style plastic bag.

Again wearing rubber gloves, triple fold and double-tie a drag rag at the middle, using three to five feet of parachute cord. When you're ready to walk to your stand, tie the cloth with parachute cord around one boot ankle, then soak the cloth with deer-attractant scent. Rarely does the rag tangle in cover if the cord is no more than 18 inches in length.

If it's a long walk to a stand, you should stop and re-apply deer attractant scent to the rag. Some hunters swear they've had good success towing drag rags with ATVs. They cover many hundreds of yards of terrain with deer scent, which presumably pulls whitetails out of thickets and into shooting range.

There are hunters who walk back-and-forth all around their stand area dragging rags in a cross or star pattern. When doing this, it's important to be certain you traverse deer trails and walk back to the stand you're hunting from. Be sure to tuck your pants legs inside your boots, and try not to let your clothing rub against brush and briers, as human scent lingers as much as deer-attractant scent.

Matt prefers not to disturb a hunting area by walking around his stand. He pulls a drag rag only when walking the path to his stand, which frequently crosses two or more deer trails, rather than walking directly down trails. He's also careful never to walk directly to a stand from downwind, choosing to approach from crosswind and "cut" as many deer trails as possible to improve the odds of a roving buck coming in contact with his drag-rag scent.

Once at a stand, untie the drag-rag cord from your boot and fasten it (still using rubber gloves) to a head-high limb well within shooting range. If there's a fresh scrape nearby, that's a choice spot for hanging a rag.

No one can tell for certain how far a buck will track a drag rag hoping to get lucky on the doe he's winded. But Matt has seen bucks follow a trail from hundreds of yards, and he believes they will track a scent a long, long way.

"Drag rags are just one more trick a bowhunter can use to tip the odds more in his favor, and it's something easy to do," he believes. "We need to do everything possible that might make a difference in getting an older, mature deer within bow range. Drag rags sure work for me, and have worked for my dad, for many years. It's become one of the important parts of our buck bow-hunting program." **>**

Matt prefers to approach a stand from cross-wind, "cutting" as many deer trails as possible, to improve the odds of a roving buck coming in contact with his drag-rag scent.

Matt Morrett, of Harrisburg, Pennsylvania, is best known as a five-time world turkey-calling champion. But he's also a dedicated bow deer hunter with over 20 years experience and more than 50 whitetails to his credit, including a 154-inch Kansas behemoth.

When to Shoot

WITH DAVE MCDANIEL

"Knowing precisely when to shoot can make the difference between a lethal hit, a cursed miss, or worse, a wounded animal."

The Missouri rut was under way, and visiting bowman Dave McDaniel felt good about a tree stand he'd set near a cornfield. A nearby pond acted like a barrier for deer traveling through the area, and a fence close to the pond formed a narrow funnel for whitetails moving to and from the corn. Dave had just seen a doe pass through the pond-fence funnel.

After 30 minutes of not much happening, Dave suddenly saw an enormous buck coming out of the corn, 80 yards away. He used his grunt call to get the deer's attention. When the buck stopped, Dave grunted again.

The buck turned toward him, and less than a minute later was within 30 yards. His head was down and he was licking his nose—classic rutting-buck behavior.

Dave grunted once more, and the buck started toward him again.

When the buck was a mere 10 yards away, Dave knew the time was right; he made his bow-drawing move. But the buck caught the motion and started to turn away. Dave gave another soft grunt that stopped the buck—glad that his grunt call allowed hands-free use. He quickly anchored his string hand, instinctively aimed, released his carbon-shaft arrow, and watched its fletches bury behind the heavy buck's shoulder.

The deer traveled just 60 yards before falling. The 180-pound (field dressed) whitetail wasn't especially large by corn-country standards. But its 18 heavy points, wide spread, and 178⅛ inches of antler mass made it one of the best trophies taken in the Midwest that year by a recurve archer.

Dave, an imposing woodsman, over six-feet, two-inches tall, shoots a 53-pound recurve bow. "When I draw, I reach my anchor, aim instinctively for a split second, then I've got to let the arrow go because the bow has no let-off, like a compound," he says. "I've got to pick the absolute best time to draw on a deer, since I don't have the luxury of holding my bow at full draw [like a compound shooter] and wait for a buck to move into an opening or turn away. With my 16-pointer, I drew at the right time, but the buck

Dave collected this massive Missouri buck because he picked the perfect moment to draw

spotted me. If I hadn't been able to grunt call and stop him, I might not have made a killing shot."

There are a lot of critical things that make a bowhunter successful, but one of the most important is the timing of a shot, Dave emphasizes. Body position of an animal is a big factor of when an archer should take a shot. Naturally, a full broadside view, with an animal relaxed, head down or looking away, is the perfect time for a bowman to shoot. But rarely is an ideal shot available to a hunter, or at least it's not attainable immediately to an archer when an animal is first spotted. Often, a bowman has got to watch and wait for a deer to move into proper position to take the best shot.

"I've turned down good deer simply because they never offered a good broadside shot inside 20 yards," says Dave. "The worst-possible body position for a bowman is when an animal is facing him. Even when a buck is quartering toward an archer, it's almost impossible to put a broadhead completely through his chest cavity, because the shoulder shields a deer's heart and lung area. An arrow shot from even the heaviest bow isn't like a center-fire rifle bullet, so an archer can't count on it penetrating a big buck's shoulder bone and entering the chest.

"On the other hand, when a deer is quartering away from an archer, that's the best time to shoot, because the chest cavity behind the shoulder is exposed well, and since a deer is usually looking away, it doesn't see bow-drawing movement."

According to Dave, for consistent archery deer-hunting success, a bowman must learn to "read" a deer's temperament or condition—"body

Anticipating where to shoot in woods terrain is an important part of knowing when to shoot a whitetail.

language," in other words. An animal that's nervous, with eyes wide, head up, and quivering hair on its back, is very difficult to take with a bow—even the fastest compound. The slightest movement by an archer or the faintest sound will spook such a deer right out of its hoof prints.

Ears also can be telling, says Dave. If they're drawn back or perked up, a deer may sense something is amiss and be ready to bolt. Foot-stomping is another sure sign a deer is wary of its surroundings—and that's no time to draw a bow and shoot. Wait, watch, and hope that deer settles down before you take a shot.

"One time, I had a good buck come by my tree stand at only 10 yards, and I never tried a shot because he was as nervous as a shad in a shark tank," Dave says. "It would have been a miracle if I'd gotten a shot at that deer. And as spooky as he was, I could have easily made a poor, wounding shot. It's smarter to pass, hoping that buck will offer a better shot some other time you're afield.

"As responsible, ethical bowhunters, we're accountable to ourselves and one another. Nothing is worth wounding an animal. It pays to be patient, and patience is one thing many beginning bowmen have difficulty learning. They work so hard to finally get close to a deer that they take a poor, low-percentage shot the first time a whitetail comes in range. Shooting instinctively with a recurve bow, I only take the closest shots at deer that are completely unalarmed.

"That's what we strive for as bowhunters. We purposely are hunting with primitive weapons, so it makes sense to wait and watch, enjoy our close-quarters hunting game to its fullest, and win in a way we're proud to remember. That's exactly why I choose to hunt with a recurve bow."

Some hunters draw their bows and aim at all deer that walk within range, studying their body language and trying to learn the best time to shoot. They practice drawing, swinging and aiming at even small yearlings and does they have no intention of shooting, insisting it will help them determine the precise time to shoot when a meaningful buck strolls into range.

"I'll often wait until a deer moves behind cover before I make my move to shoot the animal with my bow," says Dave. "You've got to anticipate whitetail actions. If a deer is coming down a trail and your open shot is on the left side of a tree, when the buck is on the right side, then steps behind the tree, that's your moment to raise the bow and draw. Be ready for a shot on the deer when it steps into the open on the left side. But, unplanned things may happen. The deer might turn and walk away, or go back out of your shooting area the way it came in. Still, planning the time for a shot before it becomes available is very important to clean kills."

It pays to be patient and wait for a buck to settle down and offer a good broadside shot, says veteran bowman Dave McDaniel.

Anticipating where and when a shot will be made on an approaching deer also allows a bowman in a stand to get his body properly positioned for it. Most bowmen stand when they shoot. Their feet should be solidly placed, body turned correctly, so when the right opportunity presents itself, a shot can be made quickly, smoothly, and accurately.

Sometimes, such little things can mean the difference between bagging a buck and going home with another tale of frustration.

There are many bowhunters whose standard tactic is to shoot when the first good opportunity presents itself. That rather simple statement is far more complex than it seems. The first good opportunity at an unsuspecting barrel-chested buck in an open meadow for a top bowhunter and skilled shot may be at 60 yards. On the other hand, it may be wise for a beginning archer to allow a skittish doe in heavy brush at 10 yards to move on without risking a possible crippling shot.

Sometimes, however, by reading an animal's actions, a good bowhunter can get a quick shot at a slightly nervous buck before the animal becomes completely spooked and leaves the area—the way Dave did with his massive 16-pointer. But don't believe an arrow shaft is quicker than a deer. If an animal detects the slightest movement or scent from bow or archer during a shot, it will bolt, which can result in a poor hit, and a long or disappointing tracking job.

When it comes to timing shots, bowhunters can expect better success by watching animals, learning their body language, anticipating where to make a shot on a deer moving down a trail, and having patience.

"Knowing when to shoot depends on the situation; there are no set rules," says Dave, with his ever-present wry smile. "You've got to go with your instincts. But when in doubt, wait things out. Never 'force' a shot at a buck with a bow." >

Dave McDaniel is a dedicated "stick bow" archer from Indiana. He has many years of whitetail-hunting experience and has taken dozens of deer shooting "instinctively" with arrows he made himself.

Let's Get Ready to RUT!

WITH DARRELL DAIGRE

"The rut is the best time to bag a big boy. Here's how to go about it."

E very bowhunter worth his skinning knife looks forward to the rut even more than Christmas. This unique, oh-so-short period is unquestionably the best time for most archers in most places to tag a better-than-average buck.

But are you really ready for the rut?

Have you planned your rut bowhunt correctly? Have you scouted sufficiently, and recently? Placed stands in the right spots? Know where to see rutting bucks and understand where they're going, why, and when?

Like most things in life, experience is the best teacher in deer bow-hunting, says Darrell Daigre of West Point, Mississippi. If you've got some prior knowledge of a wildlife-management area, farm, deer lease or other hunting acreage, you likely already know some of the prime spots to see bucks when they start moving around looking for does. If you've got no clue where to look, better put in some woods time well before rut season. Getting to know the property intimately ups the odds for rut-buck-tagging success. Locate prime, thick bedding areas. Find places with select food sources (cornfields, browse, acorns), water, and watch for last year's buck rubs and scrapes to get an idea where does and yearlings are currently living.

"A lot of times during the rut, I'll put a climbing tree stand on my back and just sort of stillhunt the best buck areas I know on the best land I can get access," says Darrell. "Frequently, especially in early morning, I'll spot a hot doe being chased by a buck or two, and that's a heck of a spot to quickly move to and climb a tree.

"The doe may circle around and come back through the area. Also, she has left a scent trail that other bucks can track, and often an hour or two later, other bucks will follow the same path she walked. That's a quick way to take advantage of the rut while bowhunting.

"I might sit in a spot where I saw a doe being chased by bucks for an hour or two. If I don't see any deer, I'll come down, put my stand on my back, and take off again looking for good areas to hunt."

When the rut "rocks," lots of good bucks fall to hunters who are well prepared, like Darrell Daigre.
CREDIT DARELL DAIGRE

Slow, methodical stillhunting is best practiced when the rut is at its peak, in places where deer are not so pressured that they're scared of their own shadows. You need a pretty good-size piece of property to stillhunt well without spooking game.

This tactic can be effective throughout the day, but Darrell likes it best during mid-day hours, so it doubles as scouting, then does his stand hunting early and late.

Field edges, old logging roads and clear-cuts are great places for still-hunting with a bow. Get the wind in your favor, move slowly, quietly, and use binoculars more than your naked eyes. Cold weather, with wind, even light snow, can be ideal for stillhunting for rutting bucks. Walk a few yards, stop, look and listen. Sit down on a log or stump periodically, especially when you have a good vantage point, like a ridge top or finger of woods overlooking a pond or grassy area. You'll hear running as bucks chase does. Watch carefully, and if you see a small buck or two on a doe, scan the near-by shadows for a bigger buck.

Top-quality optics are invaluable for this type of hunting. When a mature rutting buck hooks up with a ready doe, he'll stay with her for long duration. They may bed down side-by-side, and by looking for twitching ears, the glint of a white antler or flick of a tail, you can spot a vulnerable bedded buck with his hot babe. If you find such a love-locked pair, ease close with the wind in your favor and climb a tree. With luck, the doe may lead the buck to you, or another willing suitor may happen onto the scene.

During the peak of the rut, Darrell thinks odds of success are best by hunting high deer-traffic areas. For example, find an open oak ridge where you can cover several trails from a single vantage point. Get there early and stay there late, he advises. This is one time of year when he can get "married" quickly to a spot that "feels" good. Darrell wouldn't spend a week bowhunting the same stand, but he'd be there several times during that week if conditions were right.

"You want to see plenty of deer; the more the better," he explains.

"During the early rut, food sources like BioLogic fields are still important to deer and are great spots to bowhunt for mature bucks," Darrell says. CREDIT DARELL DAIGRE

"Don't worry if you're just spotting yearling bucks or 'skin heads' and fawns. The big boys with hat racks know the score, and sooner or later the kind of deer you're looking for will slip into view. Just use care in working the spot, making sure you're scent free and undetected."

Darrell emphasizes that he "saves" his very best buck areas for bowhunting until the peak of the rut kicks in. Then he visits those places only when the weather is ideal.

"I want a 'magic' kind of day for bowhunting my choicest buck spots during the rut," he says. "A cold, crisp day with clear-blue sky and a rising barometer is perfect, especially good if it's on the heels of poor weather with low pressure."

During the height of the rut, Darrell believes does can go "underground," because every buck on the make constantly harasses them. That's when he'll head into the thickest tangles and mucky, yucky, boot-sucking bottoms he can locate, instead of more wide-open terrain.

By locating rubs and scrapes in thickets and tangles, then knowing where does, fawns and young bucks feed, you can position stands to collect a mature buck when he makes the mistake of walking out of the jungles. Such places include field corners, hilltops and ridges, points of timber overlooking adjacent points of timber or valleys, firebreaks, old logging roads, clear-cuts, hill saddles, overgrown fence lines, the edges of young pine or fir plantations, swamp edges, necked-down trails leading across rivers and streams, even unharvested strips of corn.

"During the early rut, food sources are still important to deer and are great spots to bowhunt for mature bucks," Darrell says. "Food plots, oaks dropping acorns, fresh-cut cornfields are all places bucks cruise near because they know does can be found feeding there. Bucks often expose themselves during the early rut in food areas they otherwise would never visit during the day."

Some of the best places for rutting bucks don't look promising at the outset, says Darrell. In the core of one spot he hunts is an old woods lane that meanders through a long stand of oaks and pines. There are no well-defined trails. Tracks are hard to see in pine straw. Rubs and scrapes are scarce. If he took you there and put you on a stand, you wouldn't be happy—unless the rut was under way.

You can't tell by the terrain, but the lane is on top of a wide flat spot on a towering ridge. Off to one side of the ridge, perhaps 400 yards distant, is a massive beaver bottom and bog. On the opposite side of the ridge, some 800 yards away, is a power line planted heavily in choice BioLogic game feed.

Deer typically move back from the power line, through the timber and

Dawn is extra special during the rut, particularly for grunting and rattling. CREDIT DARELL DAIGRE

across the woods lane, then down into the beaver bog in mid-morning. They have fed and caroused in the power line area all night and are headed back to the creek tangles. The best place to see them in the open is when they cross the woods lane.

Only during the rut do they move from the bog across the woods lane toward the power line, and bowmen have collected a number of good bucks chasing does there.

Darrell doesn't know what it is about the cool and quiet of dawn through mid-morning, but the best bucks he's arrowed during the rut have come at that time. He's also had more success using deer decoys, grunting and rattling at daybreak during the rut than at any other time.

Plenty of great rutting bucks are shot at mid-day and in the afternoon. Darrell has collected some, too. But dawn is extra special, and he never misses being on stand when conditions are perfect. In most locales, hunters know the week or 10-day "window" when the rut is in full bloom. Hunting hard all day, every day makes sense, and not everyone can hunt that way during the entire rut. But when the temperature drops and it's cold and calm, Darrell will be in the woods, on stand, every daybreak.

Clacking antlers can occur anywhere at any time, but most of the fights Darrell has seen and heard have been at dawn.

"I use rattling antlers often during the rut, but I never 'blind rattle' without first seeing a big buck I want to bring in close," he says. "If I just start rattling from a hot rut stand, it could attract any number of small bucks that I don't want to shoot. If a small buck or two is lured in close by rattling, I might spook a deer, which could alert a giant buck to my location. I don't blindly use a grunt call for the same reason."

Finally, just because the rut is on, don't back off on your bowhunting skills, cautions Darrell. Hunt harder, smarter and better than you ordinarily do. It's "crunch time"—the period you've waited for all year, he says. Be determined, confident, stay in the woods as long as possible. The buck of your life may make the mistake you are hoping for, but that can only happen if you're out there hunting, working to put the odds in your favor. **>**

Mississippi native Darrell Daigre has bow-hunted whitetail deer just about everywhere possible. He's harvested over 100 animals, including eight Pope & Young size bucks, his largest a 150-incher from Iowa.

Busting Pre- and Post-Rut Bucks

WITH MARK DRURY

"Great opportunities are available to bowmen who hunt before and after the rut."

Many hunters await the whitetail rut with great anticipation, knowing giant bucks are often less cautious then, and more vulnerable to bowmen. But while archers who take advantage of lovesick bucks tag plenty of heavy-rack whitetails every season, some long-time archers prefer hunting just before and just after the hard-charging rut.

"I think the worst time to bowhunt older, mature bucks is during the very peak of the rut," says renowned whitetail expert and video producer Mark Drury, of MAD Game Calls. "During the height of the rut, most big bucks are holed up with does, not on the prowl as much as they are before the rut really begins to rock, and just after it ends."

Mark says when does are in their peak estrus heat cycle, they do not move around much. They, in effect, "hole up," and bucks don't move much after them either—which is why he feels it's best to hunt them before the main rut, then again, right after it.

So much hocus-pocus has been written about the rut, that hunters can become confused by the liberal use of scientific jargon. Some people try to dissect the rut into six or more phases, as though all deer everywhere wait for one phase to end before another begins. Veteran woodsmen know that hard rutting may take place in a region the first week of November one year, but the second week the following year, and deer just 200 miles apart may be in completely different rutting time-frames.

"I'm just interested in the pre-rut, the hard-rut and the post-rut," Mark says, "and those three phases of buck-doe activity are pretty easy to determine anywhere there are whitetails."

Mark says pre-rut action begins when scrapes are opening up in his woods hunting areas and his trail cameras record plenty of deer activity, especially older bucks. This is prime time to tag a mature whitetail.

When deer activity suddenly "shuts down," scrapes go cold, and deer almost seem to vanish, even for trail cameras, "That's the period of the hard rut, and it can last for a week or 10 days," Mark says. "I just hate that phase of hunting. I call it the 'lock-down period.'

Late-season foliage can be sparse, so post-rut stand hunters should climb high and wear camouflage that perfectly blends with a background.

"Dominant bucks stay right with estrus does, nonstop, and does don't move much," he explains. "Does simply bed, feed a little bit in the thickest cover they can find, then bed again. And big bucks are right with them, not moving hardly at all. When this happens at one of my hunting sites—and it occurs every fall—I move bowhunting locations to catch a different timing of the rut. If I'm hunting in Missouri and suddenly the hard rut kicks in, I move over to bowhunt Iowa, or Illinois. If the rut shuts down deer activity there, I'll move somewhere else, maybe back to the first location for the post-rut.

"If I give an area that shuts down a couple of weeks, big bucks start moving again, coming out of the peak rut.

"The period immediately following the peak of the rut is my absolute favorite bowhunting time. I see more mature bucks on the farms I hunt in the post-rut period, from December to the end of hunting season, than at any other time of year. Big bucks are not difficult to pattern then, because they've lost a lot of weight during the pre- and peak-rut. So they are on the hunt for food, and you can find them around crops pretty easily."

Some dandy bucks are shot long after the rut is over, when most sports-men have finished bowhunting for the season, contends Mark. The last few weeks of almost any deer season can be great, he says, because bucks and does have had time to get back into their normal schedules.

Mark says special care in hunting big bucks is needed, however, because deer begin to segregate again. Because there often are few leaves in timber tops, bowmen should climb extra high in stands during the post-rut period. Does, yearlings and young bucks herd together; bigger bucks stay alone or in small groups. Often at a hunting site, bowmen must be patient to let does and yearlings pass, then young bucks, before mature bucks show— all the while being extra cautious of the wind and their scent control.

Mark often bowhunts from ground-blind sites because leafy tree cover is so lacking late in the bow season. He says a well brushed-up natural ground blind, properly positioned according to wind direction, is often less noticeable to mature bucks than tree stands that are extra high or not well hidden in leafless timber. Mark cuts hardwood limbs while they still have green leaves, for later use in making ground blinds. He says they hold their leaves for weeks, and make exceptional blind material for post-rut bowhunting.

Late-season bowhunting can be cold, too, but it's a great time to be in the woods. There are no snakes or insects, and deer often move around a great deal because food is at a premium.

Whitetails have got to eat more in cold weather—which is usually the post-rut season. Since there aren't as many acorns, farm crops and browse plants as there were earlier in the year, it can be easier to locate concentra-tions of deer.

Food plots really draw whitetails late in the season, and Mark especially likes BioLogic fields for post-rut buck hunting. When he locates whitetails herded together near food sources, he's confident he'll find mature bucks, because while most does are not in heat, dominant bucks are still on the prowl, hoping to get lucky.

"In most northern and western states, even in Missouri, Kentucky, Tennessee, Virginia, and Maryland, food becomes a primary whitetail con-cern in winter," Mark says. "That's why I spend a lot of time hunting food sources like cut cornfields. Deer can be bunched up a good bit at this time of year, so I spend more time scouting than I do earlier. It takes a little more searching to locate deer after the rut, but once you find 'em around an abundant food source, odds of taking a decent buck are pretty good.

"Everything for me kind of comes together in late deer season. The key is getting out there and doing it. It's pretty tough to get up before day-break with the temperature in the teens, and go deer bowhunting—espe-

The period immediately following the peak of the rut is Mark's favorite bowhunting time. He sees more mature bucks in the post-rut period, from December to the end of the hunting season, than at any other time of year.

cially when you've been hunting since the early bow season, and through the rut, for a couple of months or more," Mark says. "There are fewer deer and they can be spooky in the late season. But there are some outstanding bucks shot every year when everyone else is sitting home watching football games."

Mark makes solid use of binoculars in all his deer hunting, but they're especially important to him during the late season. Because winter has killed back most understory vegetation, binoculars can be used to spot deer at long range, and the long-range locating of animals is helpful in zeroing in on prime bowhunting positions.

"Early in the season, I use binoculars to check something I first spot with my naked eyes, like movement across a field, or a brushy draw across a fence," Mark says. "But in the late season, I spend more time looking through binoculars, scanning terrain upwind of my scouting route. In this way, I locate a lot of deer that I wouldn't ordinarily see."

Mark says he likes clear, well-made binoculars that offer a wide view, so he can "sweep" an area quickly.

"I've been using a 7x45 pair of binoculars lately, and they're outstanding," he explains. "I can hold them steady with one hand because they aren't too powerful. They're fog resistant and have good-quality glass. This is important, because if you spend much of a hunting day looking through poorly made binoculars, your eyes hurt and you get headaches. It pays to have quality optics if you use them like I do for late-season hunting."

Driving or slow-pushing deer is an old standby tactic for jumping and killing good bucks after the rut. It works when done correctly by skilled bowhunters, but Mark and his brother Terry rarely drive deer.

"I'm convinced the best way to tag a big buck with your bow is to be as non-invasive of his territory as possible," Mark states. "We stay out of our hunting areas—and keep other people away, too—whenever possible, and only hunt spots when the timing is absolutely perfect. Often we'll collect a buck the first or second time we hunt that spot. This tactic has worked so well for us, that driving or even slow pushes of deer are not in our bag of tricks for bucks.

"We've been fortunate the last few years to collect some giant bucks from land we bowhunt—three scoring over 190 inches. All have been recorded on video, and none during the peak of the rut. Those bucks fell to carefully planned, non-invasive bowhunting from tree stands in the pre- or post-rut periods."

Patience and persistence are keys to big-buck bow-hunting success, but Mark believes that all a woods-man's deer-hunting skills come into play.

Non-invasive hunting techniques have worked well for Mark during the pre- and post-rut periods.

"With these skills, you have a good chance of collecting a nice buck," he says. "Without them, you're better off watching TV with your brother-in-law." **>**

Missouri native Mark Drury is a well-known whitetail bowhunter with many giant bucks to his credit, including three impressive animals that each scored over 190 inches. All three were harvested while being recorded on video.

PART FIVE

END OF
THE TRAIL

Ted Nugent's Naked-Soul Bowhunt

WITH TED NUGENT

"For Ted Nugent, bowhunting whitetails is a spiritual uplifting, a primitive rebirth of his soul."

L ight, friendly rain and pitch-black predawn sky forebode one nasty, snotty, swamp run. The steady blowing mist kept the big steel mallard weathervane on rock-solid point due west, slightly aglow in a fogged barn light.

I had the Browning 12 and a box of three-inch steel 3s already tossed in the back of the truck with my patched waders and a heap of old, beat-up decoys, excitedly turning to get the Labrador pack from their kennels when it hit me. This would be a great morning to ambush a buck on the mystical hogback ridge!

Plan B, take five!

Luckily, the dogs didn't know I was thinking waterfowl, and they snoozed soundly in their insulated boxes while I sneaked back into the house to swap shotgun for bow and arrows.

I had a hunch. It's that hunter's sixth sense, an instinctual gift that us modern gonzo rockers have to get back in touch with to maximize our primal moves. Hand-to-hand combat with the prehistoric spirit, not in conflict, but as one. Tooth, fang and claw in all its glory. And that primal scream erupts in me often. Uprising. I have learned to appreciate it and always respond.

A few precious minutes were lost in my change of plans, and now I would have to outrun the oncoming eastern glow to my favorite west wind stand set. It is times like this that a smile spreads uncontrollably, the adrenaline surges and an inner charge drives a hunter. It takes everything I've got to keep from running into myself, to remain reasonably calm and collected in anticipation of the arrival of the beast. It overwhelms. As it should.

The familiar, wet forest floor helped me maneuver the dark timber by Braille, silently, for a stealthy arrival at the huge old white oak tree my pre-season scouting had determined was the killer ambush hot spot for this wind.

Ted hunts deer literally every day of the season around the country. CREDIT TED NUGENT.

It was beautiful. My eagle-eye perch was positioned high on a massive, glacier-cut ridgeline overlooking an expansive sawgrass marsh. It offered not only access to any deer traveling the historical rutted trails on both sides of the razorback, but also a panoramic view for nearly a half mile out into the impenetrable swamp to the river.

Thank you God! You sure do grand work! It was still pitch dark, and I felt as if I belonged. Because I do.

Carefully, I tied my bow to the pull-up rope and slowly climbed aboard the elevated stimuli zone of the wild. This is how I have always gotten high. Nature surely heals, but her preventive medicine is just what the good Doctor Wild ordered.

With my full-body safety harness securely fastened, I settled in the rock-solid API tree stand for what seemed to be my zillionth vigil of the season.

This is very exciting stuff, my friends. Us hunters are genuinely moved just to be out here.

Mist in the face, air you taste, dark that envelopes, smells that flare, stirring sounds, breezes that invigorate, and those runaway visions of things to come, all make for an elixir of sensual stimuli the likes of which ain't available outside of childbirth.

Soul-stirring Spirit of the Wild stuff for warriors in the game of life.

Only a wildlife addict would sit 20 feet up, strapped in and squiggled by the gnarly embrace of a 100-year-old oak, gripping a bow and arrow with cold rain streaming down his nose.

But this is the hunter's life! After all, life is not a smooth pond upon which we gaze, but rather, snorting whitewater rapids we oughtta be breast-stroking wildly in, never missing an adventurous lick!

Couches are for Michael Jackson fans. YOWZA! YOWZA! And pass the Tedstosterone in megawads. I was goin' down for the third time. Again. I of the storm.

Sunrise never came to be. The sky went from black to a barely legal shooting light, dark gray as the precipitation slowed and birds kick-started a reluctant day.

My mental ponytail was at ritualistic full mast on its own accord, and my predator radar breathed invisible fire all around.

A hawk shared my airspace, a squirrel my supporting limb. Supersonic wood ducks whistled past my head, following the river course from a night of acorn orgy. Distant crow-speak soothed me. A doe with twin fawns cautiously picked her way deep into the bowels of protective tree-rimmed pucker-brush.

A sea of gold, bronze and yellow grasses wove artfully through black timber. Deep-green tamaracks and hemlocks protruded up from off-white dogwoods and willow, melting into gun-metal sky overhead. The dark-purple weaving ribbon of river smoked unreal fog, filtering into the whole picture. Walt Disney wishes. Ray Charles can see these graphics.

Nature breathed life into our world. I counted my blessings again. Excuse me whilst I kiss the sky.

Then I felt it. Zero warning for mere mortal cityman senses. A mystical intuition, like a mother knowing a child's thoughts. And the manifestation for a reasoning predator with a soul emerged, fangs first. Could I perform like the pure predator, my brother, the cougar? Or would the "advanced" human brain get in my way?

I dared not turn, but stretched my eyes as far left as they could possibly go in their sockets without moving my head. At first, only a mini-flicker within the screen of thick vegetation was maybe observed. The silence grew deafening. A peace blanketed the wild. A tufted titmouse landed in my face to provide a little comic relief, but I concentrated on the moment at hand. Time zoomed on, but stood still.

Then he was in the danger zone. Grooming himself at 30 yards on the wide-open trail gave me a dynamic view of his majesty. His seven-point antlers were brown, with white, ivory-like tips, crowning his handsome contrasting facial markings. He was bold. Muscled, but dainty. Cocky, yet alert. This trail had provided him secure travel for two years, and he appeared relaxed and confident. The wind did not betray me. My Mossy

Oak camo turned me into indigenous fauna. The Great Spirit accepted me and my thoughts, spurring me on.

We deserved each other.

I was well zoned. All I looked at was the crease behind his foreleg. As if Fred Bear called his name, the stag turned to look away. Perfect! My bow arm mirrored his head swing into shoot position and my arrow nock nestled tight into the corner of my pursed lips like a million times before. For a nanosecond, I blanked like a zombie, the buck distorted at the end of a distorted, dreamlike tunnel. I forced my focus back to my bow, the arrow and the deer's armpit, pulled my back muscles to the max, leaned slightly forward at the waist, and the arrow was off.

Ted hunted with a fellow Michigan native, bowhunting great Claude Pollington, to collect this heavy-horn Midwest buck.
CREDIT TED NUGENT

He nearly turned inside out trying to pivot, but the 600-grain zebra-striped projectile was in and out of his vitals before his awesome defense mechanism could outflash the 250-foot-per-second aluminum 2315 arrow, white turkey feathers vanishing into the 12 ring of his heart, perfecto! A Motown snare drum punched a beat like a Neanderthal heart's first thump.

The birds, the wind, my heartbeat, pulse and breathing, everything, stopped. The forest scrub devoured 200 pounds of venison on the hoof, pronto. I sighed. Breathing came back smoothly. A small bird returned. I could hear the river again. I rested my bow on my lap and leaned back against the damp bark in slow motion. A clockwork camo. 2001: odyssey.

My eyes stared at the point of his final departure and I pulled my facemask down around my neck, a long, deep sigh whooshing from my open, grinning mouth. I just sat there, calm, yet anxious. Smiling, silent. My watch read 8:48. The hours had gone by quickly. I closed my eyes to say a prayer of thanks and replayed the shot. No doubt the arrow was true. No need to wait. Slowly, very slowly and methodically, I reversed my morning procedure, lowering my bow and climbing down, taking it all in.

My red-coated arrow was stuck deep in terra firma, feathers blood soaked and bubbly. Confidence soared. The leafy forest blanket showed clear sign, blood spoor accenting each deep, disruptive, cloven divot. His escape trail stayed right on the game path the whole way, but I had to creep on hands and knees, snaking through the lower multiflora-rose brambles for a dozen yards here and there, giving up my Browning cap twice to unforgiving thorns.

Inches from the ground, the pungent, wet, earthy autumn smell was wonderful. I came to appreciate the role and joy of a lead wolf and his pack. Wolves and bloodhounds are truly my blood brothers. All my senses were connected and on fire.

I nearly crawled on top of him, surprised by his presence in my face. He appeared to be sleeping on his side, peacefully. His death run of 50 yards must have lasted but a flash. No more than seconds. This made me happy. Fast food in its purest form.

A flood of emotions, as always, poured over me. I sat next to him, stroking his tawny winter coat, impervious to the straightjacket briar tangle that embraced us as one, lifting his antlers in my bare hands, counting the tines twice. I marveled, as always, at this awesome, perfect package of natural, high-protein fresh flesh sustenance from the Great Spirit for my family.

More than 45 years worth of stirring memories of family hunts consumed me. Xtreme at its most intense. Ultra alive.

Many missed shots flashed back. A small, happy boy with a longbow. A smiling dad. A walk with Fred Bear. A hunt with a son.

Red dogs. A caveman at a circle of fire. A haunch roasting over fire. Paintings on stone walls. A handshake. Buffalo. A footprint in the mud at river's edge. Red braves on horseback. Leather strapped hands, bleeding, bonding two Blood Brothers forever. Black hunters dancing. Antler tips protruding from a snow bank. Wind. Circling eagle. Naked soul.

Nuge Timeline

I had the miraculous good fortune to be born in 1948, just after Les Paul electrified the guitar, and during Fred Bear's promotional campaign of the amazing challenge of the rebirth of bowhunting.

My father, Warren Henry Nugent, was bowhunting somewhere when I was born, while my mother, Marion Dorothy Nugent, was jamming with her sister Nancy on guitar for fun. I took to each of these thrilling endeavors like a man possessed from the gitgo. Decades later, both dynamos bring me spiritually exhilarating drive in my daily American Dream.

More now than ever, the creative outrage of intense rock-n-roll and the mystical flight of a hunting arrow provide me every imaginable challenge a human could ever dream of.

Like my music, my bowhunting is driven by the spirit to be the best that I can be, and there is no limit to the adventure they both provide for my soul. It is the silence, stealth, and spirituality of my sacred time afield during the spellbinding natural season of harvest with such a short-range weapon in hand that keeps me grounded and connected to the priorities of God, family, America, and work.

I hunt deer literally every day of the season around the country, and employ every legal methodology variation imaginable. I stalk, ambush, call, mock scrape, rattle, funnel, drive, bait, stillhunt, decoy, and more. It is all a thrilling challenge. I learn something new every time I step beyond the pavement, and force myself to higher levels of awareness for maximum spirit-wild absorption.

Tribe Nuge hasn't purchased store-bought meat in several decades. And we celebrate an American ThanXgiving with every precious, hard-earned meal of perfect protein from the gift of flesh from the mighty beasts. Through never-ending school, youth-organization programs, and our own Ted Nugent Kamp for Kids charity, we make it a priority to baptize as many youngsters and newcomers to the great outdoor lifestyle at every chance. This is to ensure the future of honorable hands-on conservation duty to the good Mother Earth.

Though immense fun, this hunting responsibility is a serious obligation to the land. We take it to heart and do everything in our power to counterpunch the moronic politically correct insanity that is so insulting to nature and her stewardship.

As goes the mystical flight of the arrow, so goes our souls, of this I am certain. >

With more than 30 million record albums sold, and more media face-time than most active politicians, rock-n-roll legend and dedicated bowhunter Ted Nugent has earned his status as an American icon. Acclaimed for his bold, insightful commentary on issues ranging from the American Dream to bio-diversity, he is a regular guest on top-rated television programs, and also has his own TV show, Spirit of the Wild. *Nugent is an award-winning writer—author of* The New York Times *best seller* God, Guns and Rock 'n' Roll, Kill It and Grill It *and* Blood Trails II. *As a lifelong bowhunter, he has collected many hundreds of whitetail deer.*

Fred Bear on Whitetails

"Few men had the opportunity to view whitetail deer with so keen an eye and so sharp a perspective as Fred Bear, the father of modern-day bowhunting."

F red Bear is still arguably the world's best-known bowhunter, even though he died at his home in Gainesville, Florida, in 1988. For more than half a century, his name was synonymous with bowhunting and sportsmanship. For 50 years, he built bows, designed innovative archery equipment, and bowhunted small and big game. He globe-trotted to promote his sport, making nearly two dozen films on archery and giving instructional bowhunting seminars worldwide.

It is important to remember that Fred did much of his hunting at a time when travel was not so convenient and easy. A weekend hunt pursuing whitetails was more of an outing than a mere two-day trip. CREDIT BEAR ARCHERY.

Fred collected dozens of big-game animals with his bow, including seven grizzly bears, three brown bears, seven black bears, a polar bear, moose, mountain goat, pronghorn antelope, elk, caribou, Dall sheep, stone sheep, elephant, cape buffalo, lion, and tiger. He also arrowed over 70 whitetails, his first in 1935 with a bow he handmade from Osage orange wood with string made of sinew—equipment much the same as the American Indians used.

Fred Bear was born in Carlisle, Pennsylvania, on March 2, 1902. He moved to Michigan in his late 20s and started the Bear Archery Company in 1939. Fred ran his company in Grayling, Michigan, until 1978, when the company moved to Gainesville, Florida. He stayed on in an advisory capacity, designing archery equipment and promoting bowhunting, until his death at age 86.

It is important to remember that Fred did much of his hunting at a time when travel was not so convenient and easy. A weekend hunt to the whitetail woods was more an expedition than a two-day fling. When Fred was learning his bowhunting skills, there were no portable tree stands, buck lures, camouflaged tailored clothing, nor compound bows and lighted bowsights. Scrape hunting was unheard of, and anyone caught blowing a deer call or rattling antlers would have been fodder for the loony farm.

Fred believed does are smarter, but bucks are harder to kill because they are so scared of man, they rarely expose themselves during daylight. CREDIT BEAR ARCHERY.

Fred took all his big game with recurve bows, shooting instinctively—no bowsights or any of the other innovative equipment today's archers rely upon. Although he bagged all manner of big game, he always believed the whitetail deer was the most difficult animal to hunt with a bow and arrow.

"Whitetails are the smartest of all big game," Fred told a writer just before his death. "They have learned to live with people, right in our own backyards, and the average person doesn't even know they're there. Deer are sharp enough to keep their distance from humans.

"There's no question the whitetail is the toughest of all big game to take with a bow. Their sense of smell is extremely acute. Once I was in a tree stand in a spot where I'd seen a nice eight-point buck. I'd just shot two practice blunt-point arrows from the stand, when suddenly a doe walked out very cautiously. It took her 10 minutes to go 10 feet. She looked up at me several times. But I just froze and she turned away. Deer just can't make out a person if you're still—something I don't completely understand, considering how intelligent they are. Anyway, I was in plain sight, right up in an open pine tree. I just knew she was going to spook, but I stood still and she didn't run.

"Then she saw one of my arrows. She walked over to it in slow motion, leaned way forward, and sniffed the arrow. She put her nose near the arrow's nock and recoiled like she'd been shot. She jumped back about six feet, looked around, and pointed her nose right at the second arrow, which was about 30 feet away. She made the same kind of stalk up to the second arrow, too. She was out there tippy-toeing around for 45 minutes. Then, suddenly, I heard other deer coming from behind me through the woods. They were standing almost under my feet watching the doe and my arrows, and I just knew the eight-point buck was there, but I couldn't move, couldn't do anything.

"Finally, the deer winded me and they all spooked. There was just too much of my human scent around not to eventually alert them, which is reason enough serious bowhunters should use some type of cover-up scent. That's also a good reason not to take practice shots and leave your arrows laying where deer may show up."

Fred described watching whitetail fawns cross a human trail and turn almost inside out to run away from the scent. How those young, inexperienced-in-the-ways-of-man deer knew to associate danger with man-scent Fred could not understand.

Some of Fred's most memorable whitetails taken with a bow didn't sport the largest racks. But they were hunter-wise and tough to bag.

"A hunter should be proud of any deer he takes with a bow, especially a mature doe," Fred stated. "Bucks are wary and hard to kill, but they aren't always smart. I believe a doe that has been a mother for three or four years is smarter than a buck. The buck is elusive because he's scared to death. He'll run at the slightest sound, and he'll pick out the rugged country or the thick

While he arrowed most of the world's big-game animal species, Fred considered whitetail deer the most difficult of all big game to hunt with a bow and arrow. CREDIT BEAR ARCHERY.

country to bed down. The doe is the leader, however; she has the responsibility to raise the fawns—she raised that buck when he was a fawn. She has to be alert and concerned with the safety of fawns."

Since he spent so much of his time hunting in unfamiliar country, Fred had tips for archers learning new territory.

"Scouting an area by vehicle is a good, fast way of covering plenty of ground in a hurry," he said. "Drive along rural gravel or dirt roads, field edges, anywhere deer tracks are clearly visible. Sand or mud areas are good places to locate concentrations of tracks leading to trails. Then it's time to get on the ground and walk.

"If I'm in a strange area, I like to walk around for a couple of days, still-hunting really, but with my eyes to the ground more than ahead while I look for deer sign that indicates the hottest spot—where most of the deer activity is taking place. I look for tracks, trails, buck scrapes, rubs—anything that tells me an area is being used by game. This isn't serious stillhunting, because in that type hunting, you don't spend much time looking at the ground, you look ahead for deer to stalk. When a good place to hunt has been located, I place a stand there.

"Then you have to decide how you're going to hunt it. Most of the time it's best to build a blind, or place a tree stand near a heavily used trail. This is the easiest way, and often the most productive."

Most modern whitetail bowmen hunt exclusively from tree stands, but Fred said that isn't always the best tactic.

"A great many of my deer were shot from ground blinds or while stillhunting, which is difficult, and therefore a memorable way of bowhunting whitetails," he explained. "There are a lot of places where you can see a great deal farther on the ground than in a tree. If you're in an area where you can cover a bigger territory from a tree, then by all means you should climb. But it's silly to limit your vision in a tree stand that has too many leaves and branches.

While the quantity, size, and unusual game that Fred bagged impressed most people, he always felt the kill was anticlimatic to the quest of a hunt. The time spent with friends and companions were what he treasured most. CREDIT BEAR ARCHERY.

"Some people ask why they should be concerned about deer 200 yards away, since they're hunting with a short-range bow. The reason is that there may be a hot spot for deer 200 yards away, and if you can't see whitetails moving through it from your stand, you'll never know it's there. I won't hunt from a tree stand if the area I can cover is limited."

Although the quantity, size, and unusual animals that Fred Bear bagged impressed most people, he always believed the kill was anticlimatic to the adventure of a hunt. The experiences shared with friends and companions were what he valued most. Those were what Fred reminisced about in later life more than the shooting of game. It was that side of the man, and his inquisitiveness about all things in nature, that made him unlike most other bowhunters.

Fred wrote, "Outdoor hardships are quickly forgotten. Intense heat, bitter cold, rain and snow, fatigue, and luckless hunting fade quickly into memories of great fellowship, thoughts of beautiful country, pleasant camps, and happy campfires. Trophies are not really important and have a low priority on my list. A downed animal is most certainly the object of a hunting trip. But it becomes an anticlimax when compared to the many other pleasures of a hunt. A period of remorse is in order; perhaps a few words of forgiveness for having taken a life.

"A hunt based only on trophies falls far short of what the ultimate goal should be. I like to think that an expedition be looked upon, whether it be an evening hunt nearby or a prolonged trip to some far-off place, as a venture into an unspoiled area, with time to commune with your inner soul as you share the outdoors with the birds, animals, and fish that live there."

Astronaut Joe Engle, himself a dedicated bowhunter, said this about Fred Bear:

"There's a large percentage of guys in the Astronaut Office that flat idolized Fred Bear. We idolized Fred because he represented just about everything that can be represented as a hunter, as a conservationist, an outdoorsman, but mostly a human being. Fred represented everything that is American.

"Thanks, Fred, for being an example of some mighty high goals to shoot for here on Earth." >

The late Fred Bear is perhaps the best-known bowhunter who ever lived. He founded Bear Archery, and was an inventor, world-traveling hunter, woodsman, naturalist and, most of all, a gentleman sportsman.

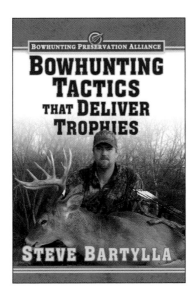

Bowhunting Tactics That Deliver Trophies
A Guide to Finding and Taking Monster Whitetail Bucks

by Steve Bartylla

Whether you're a novice bowhunter or a seasoned veteran, this book will make you a better, more complete hunter. With useful information on how to dress properly, tune and shoot your bow efficiently, find areas that trophy whitetails inhabit, and hunt those areas to maximum effectiveness from the ground or from a tree stand, *Bowhunting Tactics That Deliver Trophies* is required reading for anyone who wants to get a deer this season.

$19.95 Hardcover • ISBN 978-1-61608-674-9

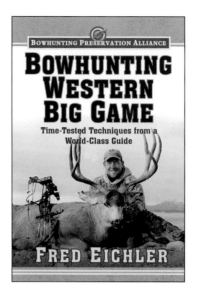

Bowhunting Western Big Game
Time-Tested Techniques from a World-Class Guide

by Fred Eichler

A master guide shares his secrets and tactics to successful bowhunting for big game in the Rocky Mountains in this essential hunting handbook. Fred Eichler, noted guide, TV host, and respected big-game bowhunter, provides readers with insight on bowhunting elk, black bear, mule deer, whitetail deer, antelope, mountain lions, and turkeys throughout the West. Although nothing is certain when it comes to hunting wild animals in free-ranging conditions, Eichler's valuable experience and advice can help tilt the scales in your favor.

Bowhunting Western Big Game is a great reference for the beginner looking for an introduction to Western game or the experienced hunter seeking advanced tips.

More than 140 photographs illustrate the game Eichler has successfully hunted in the West. Useful shot placement charts for big game and Pope & Young score sheets are also included. Suggested recipes, such as Bear Stew and Mountain Lion Backstrap with Apples and Blueberry Jam, are delicious ways of cooking your kill.

$22.95 Paperback • ISBN 978-1-62087-226-0

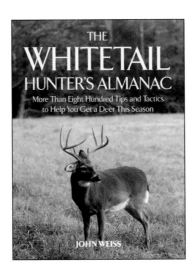

The Whitetail Hunter's Almanac

More Than Eight Hundred Tips and Tactics to Help You Get a Deer This Season
by John Weiss

To take the most impressive whitetail bucks, and to bring them in consistently, a hunter has to know his weapons, the woods, and most of all, his quarry. Now, with *The Whitetail Hunter's Almanac* at your side, you too can hunt with the strategies and practical wisdom that master hunter John Weiss has learned during his thirty-plus years on the field. Drawing on years of insider research, data studies, and personal experience, Weiss reveals the never-fail methods to making your shots count.

With careful instructions and more than two hundred photographs to bring the hunt to you, *The Whitetail Hunter's Almanac* is the must-have reference to make you a better tracker, a craftier woodsman, and a more consistently successful whitetail hunter. If you love the thrill of taking down a majestic buck, *The Whitetail Hunter's Almanac* is the guide for you!

$26.95 Hardcover • ISBN 978-1-62636-096-9

Do-It-Yourself Projects for Bowhunters

by Peter Fiduccia and Leo Somma

Do-It-Yourself Projects for Bowhunters is a detailed reference book including dozens of useful woodworking, antler, bone, and hide projects that are practical for camp and home. This guide also features articles, diagrams, and illustrations on field dressing, skinning, and quartering deer as well as information on planting successful food plots to attract game to your property. Among the many projects included are instructions for making antler knife handles, an archery workbench, game poles, tree stands, storage sheds, an archer's bookcase, bow and arrow practice holders, bow and arrow wall racks, a bowhunter's storage box, and more. Expand your hunting knowledge with complete steps to field dress a deer, quickly remove the hide of a deer, and quarter a deer.

$24.95 Paperback • ISBN 978-1-61608-816-3

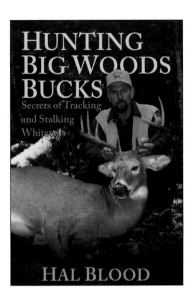

Hunting Big Woods Bucks
Secrets of Tracking and Stalking Whitetails

by Hal Blood

An extremely useful book that all whitetail deer hunters can appreciate, whether they hunt in the vast, deep woods of Maine or the cornfields of Illinois. Includes descriptions of deer and deer behavior, how to choose the right hunting gear, how to read deer sign, how to call deer, how to hunt from a stand, how to still-hunt, and details on tracking deer in any conditions.

$24.95 Hardcover • ISBN 978-1-61608-043-3